Nicole Brown Simpson

Nicole Brown Simpson

THE PRIVATE DIARY
OF A
LIFE INTERRUPTED

FAYE RESNICK

WITH
MIKE WALKER

DOVE
BOOKS

ISBN 0-7871-0339-X

First Printing: September 1994

Printed in the United States of America

Dove Books
301 North Cañon Drive
Beverly Hills, CA 90210

Contents

Acknowledgments

S pecial thanks to my publisher, Michael Viner, for his wisdom, his understanding and his infinite patience.

To my collaborator, Mike Walker, for his dedication and expertise.

To my friend and attorney, Arthur Barens, who urged me to write this book.

To Sally Nussbaum, Terrie Maxine Frankle, and Karen MacInnes for their support, their creative input, and their willingness to work around the clock. And a special thanks to Sally for keeping the laughter coming.

To Ethan for always helping with a smile.

To Mary Frann, Robin Greer, Kathy Harouche, my sister Pat Hutchison, and Kris Jenner for their loving support over the years.

To Jeanne Viner Bell for her friendship, her talents, and her wonderful contributions.

To Deborah Raffin for her warmth, guidance, and professionalism.

To Karen Fawcett for understanding and caring hospitality.

To my ex-husband, Paul, for always being there for me, and especially to my daughter, Francesca, my shining light, for her unconditional love.

I couldn't have done this without you.

Foreword

*T*o the professional thieves-for-hire who stole personal journals and photographs from my home in the wake of the O.J. murders, I say:

Attempts to intimidate me and silence me have only strengthened my resolve to write this book. Your invasion of my privacy, and the placing of phone taps at my home have literally put me in fear for my life.

I have no doubt about who sent you to steal my property: The only journals you stole were those covering the time period leading up to the murder of my best friend, Nicole Brown Simpson.

Like other friends of Nicole, I have suffered through sleepless nights, thoughts of suicide, thoughts of fleeing my own country. But I will not do any of these things. I will, with all the accuracy and all the honesty I can muster, write about the events that led up to this awful crime.

In doing this, I know I must be unflinchingly truthful about myself. Writing this book has been painful. Like most people, I shrink from exposing my innermost secrets and my most private and intimate actions. But to tell Nicole's story honestly, I must also tell you mine. Some of what I say can never be corroborated. Nicole and I had many conversations and discussed many events that were meant to be private forever, especially toward the end of her life. But on all that I hold sacred, I promise you the truth.

I know that powerful allies of O.J. Simpson will do everything in their power to discredit me. But they will fail. Because the ultimate and central fact is not me or what they will say about me; what matters is the truth.

This book is dedicated to the most wonderful friend I have ever known, and to women everywhere who are trapped in corrosive and humiliating relationships like the one Nicole did not survive. And if this book inspires even one woman to seek help in escaping the cycle of violence—what Nicole used to sorrowfully call her "little secret"—then any embarrassment I suffer will be an acceptable price to pay.

Nicole, you have no one to speak for you. Let me try...

Chapter 1

THE D.A.

*M*arcia Clark leveled her trademark power stare at me from across her desk. In the weeks and months to come, television viewers would marvel and exclaim at that steely, unflinching gaze as prosecutor Clark battled what many call the greatest defense team ever assembled for a murder trial.

"I'd like you to make a statement, Faye," she told me. "And we may want you to be a witness for the prosecution of O.J. Simpson." Then she smiled, and instantly I couldn't help feeling that, in spite of all the media hype to the contrary, here was a gentle and forthright woman. I thought,

What a formidable lady, with those wide, piercing eyes. Yet there she sits, with all the force of the district attorney's office behind her.

I was facing Marcia Clark without my lawyer, who was on business in Istanbul that day. But he'd told me, "Faye, Marcia Clark is a tough, no-nonsense lady. Just tell her the truth, as well as how you feel. You have nothing to hide. I think the two of you will get along just fine." He was right. I immediately felt comfortable as we began to talk.

I cleared my throat and leaned forward. "Marcia, I just don't feel I can make a statement right now, although I certainly intend to do so. I will gladly appear for the prosecution as a character witness. But try to understand. I need time to collect myself and to calm down. I believe my life is in danger because of what I know."

I paused. *God*, I thought, *she must think this sounds so melodramatic.* It wasn't possible to put into words the fear that had stalked me every waking and sleeping moment since that night of horror when my best friend, Nicole Brown Simpson, was butchered, along with Ron Goldman, a warm, vigorous young man. The circle of friends that O.J., Nicole, and I had moved in was now seemingly divided into two camps—those who insisted O.J. was innocent and those who wanted to see him punished for murder. I was, and am, in the latter group. As Nicole's best friend and O.J.'s confidante, I knew many devastating secrets. That is why I felt certain I was in danger!

O.J.'s head lawyer, Robert Shapiro, and his defense team had quickly surmised where I stood on the question of O.J. Simpson's guilt, character, and conduct as it related to a possible motive for Nicole's murder. And when they realized I would not be testifying for the defense, they put on the pressure. I realized then that the only way to get through this harrowing ordeal was to be absolutely candid with myself and everyone else involved in the case.

O.J.'s defense team had never explicitly threatened me. But the veiled threats behind the words they said to me in numerous calls were unmistakable, frightening. I became convinced that my paranoia wasn't merely imagined when certain pictures and documents mysteriously disappeared from my home.

Then came another horror. Word leaked to me via friends and reporters that O.J. and his lawyers had discussed floating the astounding and absolutely groundless claim that Nicole and I had borrowed money from Colombian drug dealers to open a Starbucks coffee shop, and that was why Nicole had been murdered! It's true that we'd been talking about putting up $35,000 each to open a

coffee house, but it was just talk. So my first reaction when I heard their ludicrous accusation was a
hysterical laugh. Then I began to cry. "How could
they be doing this to me?" I sobbed to my lawyer,
Arthur Barens. He suggested I make a tape in his
office for the record, which I did, using the mater-
ial from my diaries before they were stolen. These
tape recordings became the basis for this book.

In the weeks following the murders, I had the
cold comfort of realizing I wasn't the only target of
bizarre defense gambits. In what appeared to be
growing desperation, O.J.'s lawyers and "friends,"
through a series of press leaks and other ploys,
threw out one red herring after another: The
"credible burglar" who had seen two white men
fleeing from the scene—a burglar who later turned
out to be a "professional confessor" to crimes and a
convicted con man; the "racist" L.A.P.D. officer
who had supposedly planted the infamous bloody
glove at O.J.'s house to frame him; the half-mil-
lion-dollar offer for information on a "second suspect"; and the subsequent establishment of an 800
number to gather this information that proved no
more than a publicity stunt.

Marcia Clark hadn't said a word in response to
my plea for more time before I made a statement. I
leaned forward and tried again. "Marcia, I mean

what I said. I'm not trying to get out of doing my duty. But O.J. knows what I know. That's why I feel that I might be murdered."

She stood up and walked around the desk, facing me squarely. Once again, I couldn't help thinking, *My God, look at the determination in those eyes!* She smiled at me again and said, "I'm the mother of two children; I live alone. Ever since this case began, I wonder every time someone holds out their hand to me or approaches me whether I will suddenly be facing a gun, whether some nut might shoot me. I know exactly how you feel. But Faye, remember this. Nicole can't speak for herself. She needs someone to speak for her. She needs her friends now. We've talked to your lawyer, and it's not necessary for you to make your statement right away. But we're happy to know you're willing to testify for us. We'll be talking soon, I'm sure. Thank you."

I stood up, and she walked forward and hugged me warmly. I thought once again, *What a compassionate, composed human being this lady is!* My eyes started to tear. I thanked Marcia and left quickly.

As I walked through those imposing halls of justice, I was thinking of my dearest friend, my Nicole—another compassionate and extraordinary woman. But Nicole had never gained control of her life. As God is my witness, she tried desperately. When I look back with twenty-twenty hindsight, I realize she never had a chance. Standing between her and the mastery of not just her life, but the lives of her two children, was ex-husband and father, O.J. Simpson, the football superhero, the friendly Hertz spokesman, the knowledgeable NBC sports commentator, the businessman who sat on the boards of important American companies, the man beloved by millions—and a man who drew a picture of a happy, have-a-nice-day face in the "O" of his signature on his "suicide note."

But only Nicole and a few close friends and family members knew how quickly that smile, that happy public face, could transform itself into a terrifying, sweat-streaked mask of naked rage.

Chapter 2

RAGE

*O*ne of my most vivid memories—so powerful that it still haunts my dreams—is the night I saw the other side of O.J.'s happy, smiling face. When I tell you about the last times I saw that face, you'll know why I believe O.J. killed my best friend.

Nicole, O.J., my then-fiancé Christian Reichardt, and I were out on the town. I watched in amazement as "The Juice" worked his magic on adoring fans from the moment we entered a trendy restaurant called California Beach Sushi. It had a laid-back, comfortable ambiance, and the food was delicious.

It started out as one of those great, feel-good nights. The crowd recognized O.J. immediately and started dropping by to shake his hand and clap him on the shoulder. They all wanted to be next to The Juice. There was, of course, nothing unusual about this. O.J. was always surrounded by well-wishers, and he loved the attention. Soon his adoring fans had more than thirty drinks lined up for us on the bar!

Everybody was having an upbeat, noisy time. O.J. joked with the crowd. Nicole and I were chattering a mile a minute—girl talk about our friends, our kids, clothes, and future travel plans. Suddenly Nicole said to me, "Do you remember the time when Joseph…?"

The instant Nicole said the name "Joseph," she stopped abruptly. We both knew it wasn't a name to bring up. Joseph was a man so handsome, he looked hand-chiseled by the gods. He'd been the paramour of many well-to-do women in the Beverly Hills–Brentwood in-crowd, and as Nicole spoke his name, I automatically thought, *Is he still with that rock star's ex-wife he started seeing after he moved out of Beverly Sassoon's?*

Joseph had once been my lover. He had also been the lover of Nicole Brown Simpson after her divorce—and O.J. knew it. In that split second,

O.J.'s charming face turned into a profile of rage. He turned to me and burst out, "What the fuck is she doing, Faye? Why does she have to go and ruin everything by saying *that name*?" I was startled. *Why was he saying this to me?*

"Just when everything's fucking going good," he went on, "why does she *do* me like that, Faye? Goddamn! That bitch!"

I put out my hand to calm him. "O.J., please. She just said a name. It doesn't mean anything." I thought I might be able to get him to cool off, but I was wrong.

I turned desperately to Nicole. Her face was rigid with dread. She had seen this before—and she knew what was coming. "Nicole!" I pleaded, "Tell O.J. you're sorry. Please."

Nicole said, "O.J., don't."

"O.J., please," I begged, "you've got to calm down."

O.J.'s face twitched uncontrollably. His body language was extremely aggressive. Horrified, I watched as sweat poured down his face. The veins in his neck bulged. His cheekbones bunched up, twitching beneath his skin. He ground his teeth in rage and hissed at me, "Goddamned bitch! Why the fuck does she *do* this?"

I was terrified. I had to get up and get away.

Something was happening here that I only partially grasped. I couldn't believe this swift, insane anger. I hurried to the ladies' room and locked the door behind me. It was small, with just one toilet and a sink. Moments later the door burst open! O.J. had smashed the flimsy lock as if it weren't there. Before I could react, he walked to the toilet, unzipped his pants, and began to urinate! I froze, staring straight ahead at the mirror, trying not to look at him. "O.J., my God, what are you doing in here?" I gasped. "Please, get out! This is a ladies' room!"

He ignored me, continuing his noisy urination, then lashed out at Nicole again: "Goddamn her, Faye! Why does she do this to me? I never bring up Paula's name" (his ex-girlfriend, Paula Barbieri) when Nicole's around. She fucks with me all the time, that bitch! Why does she *do* this to me?"

"O.J., you've got to calm down! You've got to stop this!" I pleaded. I remember thinking how unreal this was. This all-powerful American football hero, revered by millions who thought of him as the ever-cheerful, ever-joyous, ever-grinning O.J. Simpson, was standing here beside me—blatantly urinating in my presence and cursing the mother of his children with a vengeance I'd never heard from anyone! I fled the ladies' room.

Three women were waiting to enter. O.J. cut in front of them. One angrily remarked to me, "I *know* he's O.J. Simpson. But who does he think he is?" I went back to Nicole and my fiancé. Nicole looked at once resigned, abject, depressed, and fearful. I told her, "I've got to get out of here. I can't take this! What is wrong with him?"

Suddenly, O.J. was back, snarling, cursing, threatening Nicole. "I'm leaving right now!" I said, "Christian, let's go!" Nicole, Christian, and I got up to leave. O.J. followed us downstairs and out of the restaurant, menacing Nicole and continuing to call her filthy names.

As we reached the sidewalk, O.J. screamed at Nicole, "Get in the car, you fucking bitch! I'm taking you home!" Nicole shook her head. "No, O.J., I'm not going home with you. I can't be with you when you're like this. I'm afraid you're going to hurt me."

"I'm not going to hurt you, you bitch! But you'd better get in that car. Get in the car, goddamn it!"

"No, O.J., I'm afraid! I'm afraid of you when you're like this!" O.J.'s blowup in the restaurant had apparently not gone unnoticed. Suddenly, a police cruiser pulled up in front of us. An officer said brusquely, "Are you ladies all right?"

Then he spotted O.J. "Hey, is that O.J. Simpson?" said the cop, suddenly all smiles. "Hey, O.J., are you all right?"

Nicole snapped back at the policeman, "Does he *look* all right? Do *you* think he looks all right? Is that what you'd call *all right*?" Her voice started rising, half in anger, half in fear. I, too, was terrified—for myself and for Christian. I knew that if O.J. made a move for Nicole, Christian would attempt to defend her—and I'd end up scraping Christian off the pavement.

Even with the policeman there I didn't feel safe because I was watching that O.J. magic start to work. Here was a man obviously set to go off like a powder keg, a man who looked ready to commit some act of extreme violence. But the officer was glowing as if he had suddenly been invited up into the broadcast booth to watch Monday-night football!

O.J. started what Nicole later told me was his standard routine whenever the police were called to protect her. O.J. began to explain the whole situation—still screaming, still angry, but literally trying to get the policeman on his side. He told the officer that Nicole was a rotten person. He explained the scenario, his version of what had happened. He tried to convince this cop that Nicole was at fault, that she was a terrible woman for getting him into such a state.

The policeman suddenly realized he was going to hear O.J.'s story at great length unless he broke things up. He said, "Look, O.J., you've had a lot to drink. It's time you went home. I think the best thing to do is for your wife to get into the car with her friends and for you to just go on home and simmer down."

I was horrified! Here was a policeman virtually admitting that he knew O.J. was drunk. Yet he didn't demand a sobriety test. He simply suggested that O.J. should be careful driving home.

I count a few celebrities among my friends. I know that stars get privileges and perks the rest of us don't. But I had never seen anything like this—although Nicole later told me it was a pattern she'd seen over and over.

Just because this was O.J. Simpson, he was going to get away with being drunk and threatening. Just because it was O.J. Simpson, the policeman was oblivious to that contorted mask of fury. All that cop could see at that moment was a happy, smiling face.

Chapter 3

THE FUNERAL

I walked slowly toward St. Martin of Tours, a church I knew well. It was Nicole's church. I'd attended services with her here. Emotion tugged as I thought, *This will be our final service together.* Tears welled up, but I controlled them. There'd been so many tears.

My fiancé, Christian, held my arm and guided me toward the church where we saw Al "A.C." Cowlings, O.J.'s best friend, standing outside, receiving the mourners as they filed inside.

It was the first time I'd seen A.C. since Nicole's death. I greeted him, and he gave me a big hug. Then Christian and I went inside. It was early, so we sat directly behind the rows where both families would be seated. I was numb. As I sat and waited, I thought, *How unreal this all is*. I still couldn't grasp the reality that never again would I see Nicole, or hear her voice, or laugh with her.

The day before, there had been a private viewing at a funeral home in Laguna Beach for family and very close friends. Juditha and Lou Brown, Nicole's parents, had passed the word among the inner circle, and I had wanted to attend—but I just couldn't bear it. As her closest friend, I know it was expected. Yet when the moment came to make the decision, some inner voice inside me—and it may have been Nicole's, for all I know—told me no.

One of the closest friends in our circle, Cora Fishman, a Brentwood neighbor, told me of going to see Nicole for the last time. It is so painful, even now, to think about what Cora told me.

The public didn't know it at the time, but Nicole had been nearly decapitated. So the funeral home had discreetly covered Nicole's entire body with pink-tinged white roses, neatly arranged in rows, one atop the other.

But there was another difficulty, one that no earthly hand could solve. Nicole's face showed such pain that her parents felt it would be wrong to expose her in an open-casket funeral.

I glanced up at the altar, looking directly at the casket for the first time. I knew it was a mistake to look.

I had been to many funerals. Raised as a Roman Catholic, I later converted to Judaism. I devoutly believe that there are spiritual aspects beyond death that we may never understand. Now the tears were flowing and wouldn't stop. My fiancé tried to comfort me, and I asked through my tears, "Christian, what is this all about?"

He squeezed my hand. "There's a reason for a funeral ceremony. It's a place for the friends and family to gather and sit together and share their energy. That energy force lifts up the spirit of the deceased. Soon we will be lifting Nicole up toward the astral light, to God."

It was a beautiful thought. But when he told me that, a battle raged inside me. I had the selfish feeling that I wanted Nicole here with me forever. One part of me wanted Nic to have that wonderful peace in eternal light; the other part couldn't bear to let her go.

Now people were starting to file into the church. After I got a grip on myself, I walked down and greeted Nicole's closest friends as they arrived: Cora, Kris and Bruce Jenner, CiCi Shahian, Robin Greer, and Candice and Steve Garvey. Then there were O.J.'s friends that I knew well: Kato Kaelin, Alan Austin, Alan Schwartz, and others. My nine-teen-year-old stepdaughter, Jennifer, arrived and sat with us. Finally, O.J. came in with Nicole's chil-dren, son Justin and daughter Sydney, and his two grown children from his first marriage, Jason and Arnelle.

I recoiled when I saw O.J. He looked pitiful, morbid, beaten. Yet I was disgusted. In the dimness of the church, he was wearing dark glasses. He proceeded past her casket as if he were sleepwalk-ing. He appeared to be heavily drugged. And, indeed, the press later on revealed he was under sedation.

The family arrived late. When all were seated, the monsignor began the ceremony. Again I fo-cused on the moment, on Nicole. I didn't want to cry. I'd cried for days and wanted to stop. But my grief bubbled up from my soul, unendingly. *Oh, Nicole, Nicole, how did this happen?* I thought. *How did we let this happen to you? How can I bear it without your love and your strength?*

I sent her a message, concentrating hard and sending it up into that astral light I kept imagining. *Don't worry about the children, Nic, I told her. You know I'll always be here to love them.*

In the explosion of press coverage about what they were calling "The O.J. Murders," pictures of

Nicole came flashing at you everywhere, images of a striking blonde that the press labeled "sexy" and "glamorous" and "fast-lane." Nicole was all of those things. But they were minor aspects of her persona. There was one phrase I'd use to sum Nicole up for the world that never knew her. She was a devoted, intelligent mother to her children and the most unconditionally loyal friend I and many others have ever known.

I suppose I shouldn't have been stunned at the millions of words that had been spoken in sympathy for O.J. Simpson after the brutal murders of Nicole and Ron Goldman. It just seemed so unfair that no one thought very much about the sympathy due to this woman whose life had been interrupted so brutally. *I'll find a voice for you, Nic*, I thought. *I don't know how, but I'll tell the world all about you, I swear it.*

I looked up at the family and O.J. They seemed quite composed. People started going to the altar for communion, and the monsignor benevolently invited those who weren't Catholic to come to the altar rail and accept a blessing. All of those who had come to the altar rail crowded over to console the families and O.J.

The crush of people increased when O.J. stood up and knowingly became the center of attention. They flowed toward him, shaking his hand, hugging him, expressing their condolences. At that point I went up to receive my blessing. At the altar rail I heard five-year-old Justin's (Nicole and O.J.'s son) voice from behind me. He cried out, "Aunt Faye!"

I turned and walked toward the children. Suddenly, O.J. was in my path. He looked zombie-like. It was unreal, scary. Even though I'd known this man so well, he now terrified me. He grabbed my hand and spoke in a raspy, strained voice that sounded like it came from some private hell. He said, "Girl,..." something he often called me." Girl, ...I need to talk to you, girl."

I felt like I was coming out of my skin. I tried not to recoil visibly. My tears stopped. I looked at him and said in a voice so strong it surprised me, "O.J., this is not the time. This is about Nicole."

I pulled my hand away and went straight to Justin and Sydney, trying to compose myself quickly. Justin was my special little pal. He was used to seeing his Aunt Faye's "happy face" whenever I played with him at home, helping him build little model trucks and cars and playing Power Rangers. He looked up me, wanting to see a happy face that didn't reflect all the pain and tears he was experiencing around him. But I just couldn't do it, even for Justin. I hugged him and Sydney and said I'd see them both soon.

Now the jam of people was interfering with the service. The monsignor made an announcement, saying, "Please, we must go on with the service. Could everybody *please* take their seats. This is highly unusual." People acted as if he hadn't said a word. Finally, the monsignor put a stop to it. Speaking very firmly, he said, "*Everybody* must be seated." O.J. got the message and sat down.

The service continued. Nicole's three sisters, in clear, resolute voices, gave the eulogies. I know you're supposed to say, "It was a beautiful service." I suppose it was, but I found it overwhelming. I was glad when we left the church.

Throughout the service, I'd been sending messages to that astral light Christian had spoken of, where Nicole's spirit was rising. And as I walked out of the church, it struck me for the first time what a brilliant, sunlit day it was, so unusual for June in Los Angeles, where we have what is called "the June gloom." It was silly, I suppose, to think this was a special, bright, new day for Nicole, but that's the mood that gripped me. It was as if Nicole's spirit were rising as the skies opened up to greet her.

As we exited the church, flash cameras and TV lights exploded from the crush of waiting newsmen. Everyone blinked. It was our wake-up call from media hell. We filed into limousines, and I was elated to escape from the press. Nicole hated the media attention she got as O.J.'s wife. She particularly hated cameras going off in her face, which happened often because she was such a glamorous, photogenic blonde.

Kris and Bruce Jenner, CiCi, Cora and Ron Fishman, and Christian and I rode together. The burial site was in Laguna Beach, near Nicole's family home. It was a long drive, about ninety minutes. Before long I knew that my thoughts of escaping the press had been premature. Helicopters were zooming overhead, swooping down to look into the open sunroofs of the procession, trying to spot the riders in each limousine. It was so intrusive, so depressing.

Finally, we arrived at the burial site, and that's when I felt as if we'd entered *The Twilight Zone*. I half-expected Rod Serling to appear and narrate the surreal scene that met our eyes. The helicopters continued to whirl around and above us. Packs of reporters crowded at the gates as they opened to let our procession through. I was grateful it was a gated and walled cemetery as the gates closed behind us. *Now we'd left the press behind us,* I thought. But once again, I'd find out I was wrong.

It wasn't just the media madness that made this circus so unreal. As we got out of the limos and gathered around Nicole's final resting place, I think all of us in the inner circle began realizing how strange it was that none of us was conversing. We'd glance at each other, murmur a meaningless word or a phrase, then go back into ourselves. It wasn't grief that had shut us down, cut us off from each other. It was the unspoken question that hung in the air—the dire thought we dared not speak of in this solemn place. It concerned the man who stood among us, jaw muscles clenched, isolated behind his dark glasses.

Why had O.J. masked those eyes that had stared into Nicole's soul? And then the questions: *When had those eyes last stared into Nicole's? What had he seen? And when did he see it?* None of us knew when, or how, we would consider these questions. But we knew there would be a time—and a judgment.

We assembled at the burial site. Now it was less painful to look at Nicole's casket. Somehow it seemed natural and right under the pure sunlight, which caught the grain of white-washed pinewood, Nicole's favorite. Whenever she decorated any of her homes, white-washed pine was a strong accent.

O.J. sat directly in front of the casket, so close he could have stretched out his hand and touched it. The monsignor began to speak. His words were dignified and moving. Then came a moment so profoundly shocking, so emotional, that I felt I couldn't bear the weight of my grief and anger. Nicole's mother, Juditha, stood up and read a passage, or perhaps it was a poem, that was not familiar to me. One line of it was an anguished cry for help. The words, as I remember them, were, "If anyone knows of this, please tell me now!"

It was a mother's cry for justice, a plea for the answer to a mystery. My eyes darted to O.J. Now, for the first time, I saw the power of Nicole reach out and shake him. You could see him breaking down, knowing that the moment he'd feared and fought against so furiously was finally at hand. The horror racked his body. Spasms shook him, and his jaw muscles bunched under his skin. *What are you feeling, O.J.?* I wondered. *Is it grief? Terror? Or are you thinking of yourself? Are you asking, as you did so many times when she was alive and there for you to love, "Why are you doing this to me, Nicole?"*

I walked over to him. He sat slumped in his chair. Directly in front of him, grouped around the casket, were pictures her family had collected from her home on the morning of the murders, after police let them in. O.J.'s eyes were focused on a picture that Nicole, because she loved it so much, had affixed with a magnet to her refrigerator door It showed Nicole, O.J., Bruce and Kris, Nicole's sister Dominique, Nicole's children, me, and other friends on a magical trip to our favorite getaway, Cabo San Lucas, Mexico.

I sat down next to O.J. He raised his arm wearily and pointed at the photo. "Faye," he said, shaking his head in apparent disbelief, "that was only a month ago. We were all so happy." I looked at him. I couldn't see his eyes behind those sunglasses. I said to him, "O.J., what happened?" He never moved, but again I saw the jaw muscles clenching. His lips moved. Then words that are seared into my memory forever spilled out like an unbidden cry."

"Girl...you—out of all of them—know that I loved her too much."

I was stunned. The message passed between us, crystal clear and pure as a beam of light. I looked at him. He looked back at me. I turned away from him and looked at Nicole's casket. *Had she heard?* I wondered. I knew she had. I told her then in my heart, *Nicole, they'll hear it all. I swear it.*

I walked to the casket and collected flowers from the magnificent spray of white roses that rested atop it. I turned to the women standing there and passed out five flowers, one each to Kris, CiCi, Cora, Robin, and another friend, Marianna. I kept the last for myself.

Juditha asked me to select some wreaths from those at graveside to be sent to Nicole's favorite restaurants, where she had so many friends: Starbucks, Toscana, and Rosti's.

I asked Marco, who had been Nicole's seventh pallbearer, to deliver the wreaths. Marco was a tall, handsome Italian waiter at a famous Los Angeles restaurant. He wasn't just an ordinary waiter, but the kind who could earn a hundred thousand dollars a year and pull customers in on the strength of his reputation.

When Nicole's funeral arrangements were made, the traditional six pall bearers were picked from among her friends. Nicole had liked Marco so much that she wanted to get romantically involved with him after her divorce. He was, as she would say, "worthy." But it had never happened. Marco had been terrified of O.J., knowing his habit of suddenly appearing at restaurants when Nicole had a date and making an unwarranted scene. A few eyebrows were raised at the idea of a seventh pall bearer, but I told Marco, "Nicole would have enjoyed this. You know how she loved to flip people out."

Now I turned to say good-bye to people I knew would not be going on to the gathering at Nicole's parents' home. Then I went to the casket, touching it for the last time in farewell. I walked over to a beautiful tree nearby, away from the crowd. I took out two cigarettes, one for me and one for Nicole. My spirits lifted for the first time as I lit mine. It was our final act of rebellion together.

O.J. had never allowed Nicole to smoke in public, so she'd have to sneak off to have a cigarette, and I'd go with her. It was the kind of thing women do, girlfriends covering for each other in a male-dominated world that always told us to be "good little girls."

I smoked my cigarette and put it out. Then I took Nicole's cigarette and placed it at the base of the tree. As I walked away, I looked up and said, "Hope you enjoy it, Nicole."

Suddenly a new shock—I found myself staring straight at more than a hundred reporters and photographers, who were hanging over a low stone wall at the back of the cemetery, pointing their cameras and clicking away furiously. This time, I had to laugh. I looked up again and said, "We got caught, Nic. But at least this time, they can't get your picture."

* * *

We drove to Juditha and Lou's house in Dana Point. The minute I walked into the house, I saw what was happening—the two distinct groups had already started forming: the O.J. camp and the Nicole camp. O.J. and his cohorts were holding court in the living room; Nicole's friends were gathered in the courtyard, a vantage point from which every room in the house could be observed. As I gathered with them, the unspoken question still hung in the air: *Did O.J. kill Nicole?*

Now we started to talk among ourselves, not bringing up the question directly, but slowly saying things that were moving in that direction. Then we realized that this was not the time to speak. O.J. had six formidable bodyguards who looked like Secret Service men. They even wore those tiny black earphones. Now they filed out into the courtyard to stand among us. And as we began to speak, they moved toward us in a way that was subtle but, to me, unmistakable. Somebody had sent these bastards out to eavesdrop, to hear what we were saying about O.J. Simpson.

I was furious. We all were. I shot a glance through the window that looked into the living room, where O.J. was acting as if he was an emperor of some obscure kingdom. I thought I saw him looking back at me, but it was hard to tell with those ridiculous dark glasses. I wanted to leave. I was so angry that I had to endure this manipulation. I looked around for Kristian, but suddenly a commotion started.

Helicopters whirled overhead. In the living room, an intense phone conversation was going on as the O.J. group listened, concern written on their faces. The phone was slammed down. A rumor swept through the house that a warrant had been issued for O.J.'s arrest. Was it true?

I watched through the window as O.J. and Al Cowlings got up and went into the master bedroom, closing the door behind them. Kris Jenner said, "Look at that. O.J. and A.C. are going to do the same stunt they've been pulling for the past twenty years. Whenever O.J.'s in trouble, A.C. is there to cover for him. Now they're going to change clothes. That's what they do when O.J. wants to get away from somewhere unnoticed."

Moments later O.J. walked out—and then I realized how right Kris had been. It wasn't O.J. It was A.C. in O.J.'s clothes. He swept out of the house surrounded by security guards. The noise of the buzzing helicopters followed Cowling while O.J., in Cowling's clothes, slipped away unnoticed.

Chapter 4

FIRST MEETING

*P*ain. That's where this story started. It was the pain I saw on Nicole Brown Simpson's face when I first met her. It was 1990. Kris Jenner was staying at my home during her divorce from Robert Kardashian. At the time, I was married to a terrific guy—Paul Resnick, a wealthy businessman. One morning as we sat having coffee, Kris made a phone call to O.J. Simpson.

From the conversation I overheard, he and Kris were talking about how Nicole did not want to talk to Kris. Apparently, this was because she had heard Kris had been having an affair during her marriage to Kardashian. After Kris hung up, she explained to me that Nicole was a free spirit in many ways, but she did not condone people having extramarital affairs. Nicole was adamantly against infidelity because O.J. had bedded women every chance he got. Nicole, Kris told me, had never fooled around on O.J. during their entire marriage.

It disturbed Kris that Nicole was upset. "I'm going to go talk to her," she said. "Come with me, I want to introduce you. You and Nicole are very similar in a lot of ways. I think you'd get along really well."

We drove over to O.J.'s estate on Rockingham. It was a fabulous place. As we drove through the gates, I thought, Hertz must pay this man major money. The housekeeper let us in, and Kris said, "Let me show you the pool; it's beautiful."

We strolled the grounds. They had been laid out by Nicole with extraordinary taste—a large play area for her children, an oversized pool surrounded by rock landscaping and a waterfall slide. The house itself had a beautiful country-like interior. It was evident that Nicole Simpson was a talented interior designer.

A cheerful female voice yelled from inside the house, "I'll be out in a second." I looked up toward the second floor where a beautiful woman had appeared on a terrace.

It was Nicole. She had been in the shower and was wrapped in a towel tucked above her breasts. As she lifted her arms to remove another towel wrapped around her head and shake out a mane of fine blonde hair, her long, athletic legs and incredible muscle tone were evident.

Then she came down from the terrace, and Kris introduced us. Nicole looked at me directly with frank, laughing eyes. She smiled, showing another major asset, those white teeth. This woman looked like an angel.

But as we chatted, I felt a guarded quality. I looked into her eyes more intently—and I saw it. Pain. I just chalked it up to the pressure of being married to a celebrity. After a few minutes, I walked away from Nicole and Kris to survey the grounds, knowing they needed a chance to talk.

Before long, they rejoined me as I admired a flower bed. We talked for a while, then Kris and I left. As we drove back to my place in Beverly Hills, I said, "My God, she's so beautiful, and she seems like a warm, good person. But she's having a hard time, isn't she?"

"Oh, yeah, she's having domestic problems," Kris answered.

She didn't say anymore, so I wasn't sure what that meant, and I didn't ask. Whatever had caused the pain I saw in that woman's face must have been a fearful thing to endure.

* * *

Several years later, on a New Year's trip to Aspen, Nicole and I were house-guesting at a friend's, and I told this story to a young guy she had become romantically involved with after her divorce. Nicole overheard the conversation and came barging into the room.

"How can you say that about me?" she scolded.

"Nicole, it's true. That's what I saw in your face. You don't look that way now—but can you tell me you're the same person today that you were back then?"

"No," she admitted. "How could I be? I was clay, and O.J. sculpted me the way he wanted me to be. I was this seventeen-year-old girl serving platters in a restaurant, and the great O.J. Simpson changed my personality to reflect his idea of the perfect woman. I was his creation."

For most of the time I knew her, Nicole's life was rebellion. She kept trying to find a way for that shining spirit of hers to peek out from behind the formidable shadow of O.J. Simpson. And sometimes her way of rebelling was to freak people out.

It would be things like this: They'd have a big gathering at their house. She'd walk over to O.J. and say loudly, "Excuse us please—we're going to the bedroom and fuck now."

The funny thing—and Nic and I used to laugh about it—was that O.J. never realized it was her indirect way at getting back at him, of rebelling against his pervasive power over her. He just thought, "Hcy, this girl can't live without me." And he'd wink at everybody and echo her words with a broad grin saying, "Excuse me a minute, I'll be right back."

* * *

I didn't see Nicole for a long time after our first encounter. And I never met O.J. until the day I ran into the two of them at Suzanna's, one of my favorite designer shops. Nicole's daughter, Sydney, was just a baby then. So after Nicole introduced me to O.J., I sat in the little coffee area Suzanna maintains for her select clientele and admired the pretty child.

In those days, O.J. acted courtly and admiring toward Nicole. I thought, *How nice*. They seemed like such a loving couple. But as we talked, I noticed how he concentrated on charming me, almost pushing Nicole into the background and talking only about himself. I soon discovered that the key to O.J. Simpson was simple: He had it all—but he always wanted more. His need was to dominate, to be the center of attention whether he had an audience of one or a million. His public life and public image were all-important, as was his effect on individual women. Celebrity sports tournaments, "A-list" parties, dinner gatherings of the rich and famous, personal appearances and interviews, tête-à-têtes, and liaisons with single, desirable women—these were the ingredients of O.J.'s lifeblood.

As I got to know them better, I realized that Nicole wasn't the woman he needed. O.J. wanted a wife who was beautiful, and Nicole filled that bill. But he also needed someone who loved accompanying him to celebrity and social functions, a decorative female who would never intrude enough to steal the spotlight, a woman who would adore him unreservedly. O.J. Simpson wanted a Barbie doll that he could call his own.

Nicole hated the Hollywood scene, the social game-playing. But sadly, she was in love with an American football hero who was now a Hollywood man. That fatal flaw ate away at their relationship. It fed O.J.'s secret and egocentric view that she was inadequate, and it gave him a made-to-order excuse to womanize.

O.J. used to tell me, "If only Nicole would go out with me more. If she would be there for me. She makes such a big deal about hating this Hollywood scene. Why can't she just do it for me?"

I heard a different message, the sound of a woman fighting to be her own person. I found that out as we became friends. And it's strange that we became so close, because I'm a woman who loves shopping and social events—and spending more money on hair and nail appointments than I care to mention. Nicole dreaded shopping and going to other people's gatherings. But she did love throwing at-home dinner parties and dropping in at Hollywood hot spots like the Roxbury and Bar One to dance and have a couple of drinks with friends.

As I got to know Nicole, I learned about her history and discovered that she'd actually been born in West Germany. One touching remnant of that childhood is the way Nicole recited the Lord's Prayer to her children every night in German. Nicole's mom, Juditha, had met Lou Brown, Nicole's dad, in Europe when he worked for the famous U.S. military newspaper, *Stars and Stripes*.

Nicole and the family moved to the United States in the 1960s, and she grew up as a California girl in the middle-class town of Garden Grove. She crowned her school years by winning the title of Homecoming Princess at Dana Hills High School. Nicole and O.J. met in 1977 when she was just seventeen. He was still married; she was working as a waitress at The Daisy, a Beverly Hills hot spot. O.J.'s marriage eventually ended in divorce, and, after years of being together, they married in 1985.

It was an interracial marriage, but that was no problem for Nicole or her family. O.J. quickly turned himself into a favorite son, setting Lou up in his Hertz dealership and helping Juditha and other family members in various enterprises.

O.J. was generous to a fault with Nicole. She got an allowance of somewhere between $5,000 and $7,000 a month, and O.J. showered her with gifts. They owned homes in New York City, Beverly Hills, Laguna Beach, and San Francisco. And they constantly jetted off for deluxe vacations at resorts in Florida, Aspen, and Mexico.

I'd read about Nicole before I met her. She was always in the papers, usually at O.J.'s side and routinely described as "O.J.'s gorgeous, blonde wife." Even before I really got to know Nicole, I heard from mutual friends over and over that she was a super-mom who did everything for her kids.

Friends who knew her well said she had the typical California beach-girl approach to life, casual and free-spirited. What I also heard from people in the know was that O.J. treated her like his prize possession. He would fly into jealous rages if he even thought another man was looking at her. This caused a few problems because Nic's favorite recreation was dancing. Whenever she got out on the dance floor—dressed in ripped jeans topped by a midriff-baring T-shirt or tank top—admiring males crowded around to watch.

Most of all, Nicole loved her home and loved her children. As someone who works hard at being a good mother, I know another one when I see one. I'm very active in the PTA and drug-education programs, and I've sat on the Board of the Beverly Hills Education Foundation. I'm an art docent at my daughter's school and have donated time and money to children's charities. I know what a good mother is, and Nicole was sheer perfection. The children came first with her always.

I'd call her up and say, "Nic, let's go to Starbucks for cappuccino," or, "Let's go to Rodeo Drive; you have *got* to get some clothes."

She'd inevitably say, "Oh, Faye, I just can't, I've got to take the kids to..." She took them everywhere—dance class, karate class, the zoo, the park, for ice cream, to kiddie parties. And at home she'd play games with them for hours or read story books to them. That was Nicole's life, but that also caused problems with O.J.

When O.J. asked her to travel with him to New York, or Florida, or wherever he pursued his career, Nicole would often refuse. That's when O.J. would start complaining that she never wanted to be with him. He couldn't understand that when a woman has children you can't just separate her from them. You've got to maintain a home and a schedule for kids.

O.J.'s response was to use Nicole's devotion to home and children as a justification for straying. How many times have I heard O.J. say, "There are fifty million women out there who want O.J. Simpson." If Nicole wasn't going to be with him, O.J. felt he had the right to find some temporary substitutes.

O.J. loved Nicole's superb body. Her girlfriends used to marvel at her muscle definition. She ran about nine miles a day, usually with Cora Fishman, whom she used to meet every morning. I was never able to run with them because I have an on-going knee problem, although I work out regularly. But I would catch up with them at Starbucks coffee shop in Brentwood, a short drive from Beverly Hills, where a group of young good-looking guys hung out. We called them "The Starbucks' Boys." That's where Nicole first met Ron Goldman.

As I set down these personal thoughts, my own private diary of the friendship I shared with Nicole, one of my hopes is to correct inaccurate press reports about who she was and what she stood for.

Some newspapers, for instance, said Nicole was a regular at "The Gym" in Brentwood. That's false, if harmless. Nicole went to the Pro Gym, where Ron Goldman worked out. One of the most shocking press reports—which relates to O.J.'s hatred of Nicole getting fat during pregnancy—was the one that said she'd undergone six abortions because she didn't want another child with O.J. That report, alas, is true, a testimony to both her devotion and her fear of him.

In the wake of the murders, what struck me as bizarre was the almost total absence of in-depth stories about Nicole. O.J.'s life has been examined and re-examined with excruciating thoroughness. Nicole is dismissed as O.J.'s sexy-looking wife. Now, more than ever, I'm aware that in criminal cases involving a woman, there's always the tendency to hint that she's probably guilty of sluttish behavior—even when she's the person wronged. Please understand: Nicole Brown Simpson was the victim—not O.J.!

In 1992, during a party at Kris and Bruce Jenner's house, Nicole flashed a peace sign at me, which was her usual way to avoid problems with O.J. and friends. I'd been acting jealous and stand-offish because she'd shown up with handsome Joseph Perrulli, a man I'd once romanced. The peace sign was pure Nic, saying, "Let's be friends." This was after she had divorced O.J. The court had awarded her a lump sum settlement of about $450,000, $10,000 a month in child support, and a luxury condominium at 875 South Bundy Drive, not far from O.J.'s home.

I was divorced from Paul Resnick, my third husband, and in a new relationship with Christian Reichardt, a chiropractor. I was managing his office, which was near Bundy Drive, so I'd usually run over to Nicole's just before lunchtime. By then, she had returned from her morning nine-mile run and coffee at Starbucks.

We'd go to lunch at one of our favorite spots—Toscana, Rosti's, or Sushi Boy. Sometimes I'd take the afternoon off to go shopping in Beverly Hills, but Nic would rarely come along. Shopping just wasn't her thing. But sometimes Cora and our pal, CiCi Shahian,—a real fashion plate—would gang up on her and insist she needed new clothes.

Most afternoons, Nicole hung out with her kids, watching—with enormous love and fulfillment— as they splashed in the pool, or laughingly chased each other around the grounds. Nic was a sun goddess, an outdoor girl, and they were her cherubs.

After leaving O.J., it tickled her that she could be comfortable and casual at home. At O.J.'s house everything had to be in order, a syndrome I knew well from my Germanic stepfather, where every towel, every washcloth, every book and picture had to be in its proper place, geometrically aligned.

O.J. was just as meticulous, compulsive really, with his clothes. His closet space was as big as any woman's. He'd change clothes several times a day, refusing to wear anything that was the slightest bit wrinkled.

I'm more like O.J. in that respect. Every time I came over to Nic's house, I'd be picking up clothes, toys, and wet towels, or stacking dishes and tidying the sink. "God, Nicole," I'd laugh, "This place is a mess. The kindest thing I can say is that you're rebelling against O.J." Nicole just shrugged and said, "Children have to play."

When Nicole first served the divorce papers on O.J., she suddenly stopped talking about him. This strange silence about a man she'd lived with for seventeen years baffled me. It continued until her fateful decision to attempt a final reconciliation in the spring of 1994.

Many times I asked her, "How do you just switch from one life to another without ever referring back to it?" Even though I'd been divorced from Paul Resnick for years—and we certainly had problems—I still have fond memories. Even now, we remain dear and loyal friends.

There are good times in any relationship. But Nicole never spoke of such memories. An as our relationship grew closer, she'd make vague references about abuse by O.J., but it was a long time before I heard the awful truth. That's how O.J. Simpson got away with what the world now knows was continual, savage abuse. Nicole rarely talked about it.

After the divorce, whenever she was out in public, people never knew her identity as O.J.'s wife unless someone else told them or they figured it out for themselves. If anyone asked her who she was, she would say, "I'm Nicole Brown," never, "I'm Mrs. O.J. Simpson."

As she admitted, O.J. had "molded" her, but she never needed him to validate her identity. She was proud and content to be what she was—a wife and a mother.

Once she was separated, men started looking at her differently. She'd always been gorgeous and sexy, but men around Brentwood and Beverly Hills knew that O.J. Simpson wouldn't tolerate anyone messing with his woman. Now she was fair game, and she knew it. Just about every man she came in contact with was attracted to her.

I remember when Nicole realized at last that it wasn't forbidden to look at men romantically. One day the law firm handling her divorce sent over a young—and I mean young—law clerk named Brett Shaves. He had some papers for her signature. Brett couldn't take his eyes off Nicole.

Nic told me about Brett during a phone call when I was in Europe. We broke out giggling like a couple of schoolgirls when she told me he was just twenty-nine. It was refreshing to hear Nic laugh—and stimulating to see her blossom under the admiring gaze of a handsome young man. And Brett was handsome.

But it was not Brett whom Nicole took as her first lover after filing for divorce. It was Marcello, her hairdresser. Nicole started dating him in the summer of 1992. They'd go out for dinner, then drinks and dancing. And one night Nicole decided to "do" him—the euphemism in our circle for a sexual encounter.

I should explain, by the way, that there's another phrase we use when sex doesn't include actual intercourse. We call it "playing." Nicole had a theory that if she didn't have intercourse, it wasn't really sex. She liked to play.

I remember one night after her divorce when we had gone to Roxbury, met up with some friends, had our share of tequilas, and reached the giggly stage. After Nicole and the group dropped me off, they passed the house of a neighbor she had been eyeing for quite a while. He was black, great-looking, and seemed totally absorbed in his fiancée and his studies at an Ivy League college. But that didn't stop Nicole. His roommate was driving the car, and Nicole suggested that they stop in for a drink.

While the others sat with their drinks, Nicole quietly slipped out of the living room and into his bedroom. He was sleeping, so without taking off her clothes, Nicole gently pushed the covers aside and teased him into an erection. Without suggesting that she wanted anything in return, she gave him what she later described as "a lovely surprise—the blow-job of his life."

The next morning she reported that she had giggled all the way home, because as she left, he looked up and said just one word, "Thanks." She added that she knew he had wanted her for a long time but was too fearful of O.J. to make a move in her direction. Nic had done it again. She loved to flip people out. We later referred to that episode as her "Brentwood Hello."

In the summer of 1992, Nic shared a romantic weekend with Keith Zlomsowitch, a manager for the company that owned Mezzaluna restaurant and the Monkey Bar in Los Angeles. Nicole was strongly attracted to Keith, and she was vulnerable, the way we often get—men and women alike—after we shed an old relationship. One night, after they'd been out dancing, she decided to "play" with Keith.

Everyone has heard the 911 tape in which O.J. inadvertently reveals that he stalked Nicole. It was this night in 1992 that he was referring to when he screamed about catching her "playing" with Keith. It had been one of those evenings when O.J. hid in the bushes and spied on her. He'd been doing that almost from the first day of their separation. Nicole and I called it the "Bush Syndrome." This time it was around midnight—and O.J. watched through the living-room window as Nicole performed oral sex on Keith Zlomsowitch.

I decided I'd better try to diffuse the situation. If I got O.J. mad, he might get violent, and I didn't want Keith hurt. So I tried to calm O.J. by saying it wasn't going to look very good if people knew he was spying from the bushes. That really got to him. O.J. could not stand to see his public image hurt. He began acting civil to Keith and told him he wouldn't hurt him.

Toward the end of her life, Nicole sometimes seemed powerless to help herself as O.J.'s obsession for her mounted to an insane crescendo. And even in 1992, people who knew them fairly well wondered how Nicole had gotten him to agree to a divorce. What people forget is that O.J. had been charged with battering Nicole after police found her cowering outside her house in 1989, badly beaten and dressed in only a bra and sweat pants. O.J. did not want a repeat of even the minor media stories published about that incident.

In the 1989 case, O.J. pleaded no contest. The judge sentenced him to two-year's probation. That meant that if he was caught beating Nicole again, he'd probably do jail time. And, as everybody now knows, Hertz considered dropping him as their spokesman. Nicole saved O.J. by getting on the line with one of their top executives, swearing that it had been no big deal.

So from 1989 to 1992, Nicole sometimes had the power. O.J. felt vulnerable after his close brush with disaster. That's probably why Nicole was able to stop him from doing violence to Keith. And needless to say, she and Keith ended their romance. The poor guy had been scared half to death. He and Nicole remained friends, but were never together sexually again.

Talking about that awful night with Keith in 1992, Nicole said, "When I told O.J. he had no business interfering with my life, he turned it around and said he was concerned that our kids, who were upstairs sleeping, could wake up and walk downstairs. He said it was the wrong thing to be having sex with the kids in the house."

I quickly countered, "That's ridiculous. Most people with children have sex in their own home when the children are sleeping! And when the hell did he get so concerned about the kids! From what I've seen of O.J., he spends very little time with them. Even when he has them for the weekend, he usually calls up long before it's time to bring them back and tells you to come get them because he can't take it anymore."

Here's the truth about O.J. and his children: Once Nicole left, he rarely saw them. He'd be out of town three and four months at a time—and seldom called to speak to them. When he was in town, he would say he was taking the kids for a weekend, but he'd bring them back that same night.

The kids also served as O.J.'s made-to-order tool for manipulation. Whenever he had the kids and heard from his pals around town that Nicole was out having a good time, he'd contact her and say "I've got to bring them back right now."

He constantly tried to ruin every opportunity for Nicole. I remember many times when we'd have to cancel plans to go out for an evening because O.J.—who was supposed to be taking the kids—would call at the last minute and say, "Something's come up, I just can't take them."

The saddest incident of all, one that broke my heart, occurred when Nicole and O.J. attempted a reconciliation in the last year of her life. I heard their daughter, Sydney, say to Nicole, "Mommy, I don't want Daddy to come back. Why do you want Daddy to come back? I don't want all the fighting to start again, Mommy."

That's when Nicole told me Sydney had a sleep-walking problem. Nicole believed it was because Sydney's bedroom was right next to her parents' and she heard the beatings, fights, and squabbles. I love Sydney just like my own child, and every time I think of how panicky she must have felt, I start to cry.

Little Justin was too young to understand most of what was going on, but it's sad to think that here's a little boy whose daddy was a sports super-star—and yet, Nicole told me, O.J. rarely played catch, or Frisbee, or wrestled in the grass or on the floor with his own son.

Chapter 5

FAYE'S CHILDHOOD

ACROSS AMERICA
1957–1985

I am so afraid for Sydney Simpson. At age nine, she has been aware of all the violence O.J. brought into her home. I fear that, like her mother, she has become adept at blocking out evil memories, and that one day she's going to explode under the pressure of it all.

I often think that one of the reasons Nicole and I bonded so powerfully, literally becoming soul mates, was because I identified with the abuse she suffered. It's painful to write about this, but it may be one of the reasons I've been driven to set down Nicole's story as I know it. I was an abused child, and I think that the fear and powerlessness that comes from never having a safe haven makes such children extraordinarily alert and aware. Sadly, abused children are forced to become wise little souls.

My mother was of Spanish and Italian descent. She married into a very proper family that boasted English forebears in the Deep South. When she talks of that life, which I never experienced, my images are of a southern manor house, complete with servants, affluent-looking men who smelled of cigars and whiskey, and beautifully dressed women with soft, southern voices.

When my mother was pregnant with me, my father abandoned her and my three brothers and sisters. It wasn't until I was an adult that I learned he had been an alcoholic, and his disease wouldn't allow him to deal with the pressures of being a father of four. Because my mother never told me the truth, I developed a guilt complex, thinking that my impending birth was the catalyst that led to the breakup. So much for keeping things from children. If you shield them from reality, the danger is that they'll construct a scenario that ends up harming them more deeply than the most painful truth.

My mother met my stepfather when I was four. At the time, she was supporting us by working as a nurse and attending journalism courses at college.

Supporting four children and studying left her precious little time for us. She was a dedicated lady, and she managed to make a good home. Whenever my mother would come home, I would hang on to her skirt and follow her everywhere she went. She was my security, all I had. Then she married my stepfather. Now, in addition to working and going to school, she had a man in her life. There was no time for her children anymore.

The man my mother married was an ex-paratrooper, a Germanic man who believed in perfection. He wanted his house and family kept in apple-strudel order. We had to be little perfectionists, just like him. That's when the woes began.

For example, I was a bed wetter. My mother, not knowing any better, tried to treat this problem by giving me castor oil every night. My stepfather decided that I was wetting the bed as a ploy to get attention. One week after he married my mother, he started spanking me every morning.

At age four, being spanked for wetting the bed made me feel even worse about myself. I had no control of my problem, and far from using it to get attention, I hated wetting the bed. Who wants to wake up in a wet bed? But now I had to face an automatic beating every morning. I didn't want to sleep at night because I was afraid to wake up.

My life became hell. At first, my stepfather spanked me the way you would spank a child. But as I grew older, and my mother allowed him to take more and more control of us children, the spankings became hideous beatings. I would scream, "Mom! Mom!" My brothers and sisters would run to her and cry, "Mom, he's beating her! He's hurting her! She's got bruises!" And my mother would say, "Well, there's nothing I can do about it. Your father knows best. And he feels she's doing it intentionally. He feels he can spank it out of her."

My mother had a dog named Candy, a little poodle. At five o'clock each evening, when my stepfather would come home, Candy would bark to warn us. Although we had the house in spic-and-span condition as he demanded, we'd all scatter in terror. Then we'd sit down and start doing our homework furiously, trying to be the perfect family for him. Whenever I think of my mother during this period, the only clear picture I have is of her pecking away at the typewriter in her office. That's what she'd do while my stepfather rampaged through the house, threatening and beating her children. We felt completely unprotected.

My father was an executive for a book company. His job was to start up book stores, hire the sales people, and get things running properly. Then he'd move on to the next town and do the same. We were always moving. I attended about thirty different schools, and, believe me, being the new kid in school thirty times is no fun. But it did make me less inhibited, and I think that was a good thing.

As I grew into my teenage years, my mother became quite successful as a journalist. In every new town, she would get a job writing a column for the local newspaper. Most of the time she wrote about issues of interest to Spanish communities. Mother became an activist for Latino causes. She felt she had ignored her own culture when she was a young woman, so she wanted to write for other women of Spanish descent and inspire them to be proud of their culture.

I remember when we were living in California she was writing a column called "La Catora," which means "The Parrot." She'd write the column in English, then translate it into Spanish. She became very well known in her field after she turned to holistic medicine. As a holistic doctor, she published many articles on the subject. Mom's quite a lady; I'm proud of her in many ways. Even though she didn't know how to be a mother, in spite of having seven children, she did her best.

Just to make my childhood even more chaotic,

my mother turned into a religious fanatic. Once a devout Catholic, she joined the Jehovah's Witness movement. So I was raised thinking that the world would end in 1975—that Armageddon would come when I was eighteen years old. I think that's why I had my first sexual encounter at sixteen—I didn't want to miss the experience before The End.

God had other tests in store for me. At sixteen, I left home to live with an aunt in California, where I graduated from high school. I worked as a bank teller and, briefly intrigued by law, took some legal courses in Chabot Community College. But the law was not my cup of venom.

When I was named "Miss Hayward," it gave me both an ego boost and some career ideas. They led to finishing school courses and eventually the successful directorship of a John Robert Powers finishing and modeling school.

Married for a short time, then divorced, I moved to London and married an eccentric heir. Our child, Francesca, was born when I was twenty-seven, and we lived the best of lives on two continents in London, France, and Australia.

That marriage, too, failed. I came back to the United States, married Paul Resnick, and volunteered as a fund-raiser for children's charities. We lived in Beverly Hills, and although Paul and I also divorced, we remain the best of friends.

I have been in the Betty Ford Clinic twice and the Exodus Recovery Center once over an eight-year period for cocaine addiction. I honestly believed that I had beaten it after my second Betty Ford trip, but the pressure of watching Nicole's tragedy unfold weakened me. That is not an excuse; it's just an opinion.

The last time I talked to my mother was in 1992. She admitted to me then that she didn't undergo that mysterious experience called bonding with any of us children. She said, "I knew you were my children, but I just didn't have a special feeling." That floored me. When my child, Francesca, was born, I felt the same way. Even though I'd been so careful during my pregnancy not to smoke or drink, to make sure I had the perfect child, when Francesca was put into my arms, I didn't feel that special closeness—and it terrified me.

After hearing this revelation from my mother, we contacted my grandmother—and she said she never felt this way about her children either. She told us that her mother, too, had felt the same absence of bonding. This was a chain that had to be broken. I'd always been worried that somehow I would end up not bonding with my child.

It's typical to carry on the cycle, and I'm happy to say that it ends with me. I have never struck my child. What's more, I have taught her that bringing a child into the world is a precious and rewarding act, one that enriches the mother and contributes to the perpetuation of humanity. I have immersed myself in her life, and I've made certain there's always a safe haven for her. That's a promise to her that I can keep. And it's a promise I'd like to keep for Nicole's children.

Chapter 6

THE LOVERS

Nicole's love life after O.J. started with Marcello, a protégé of a world famous hairdresser. Marcello had been a friend of mine even before he met Nicole and actually introduced me to my then-fiancé, Christian Reichardt.

Marcello has the good looks of an Italian movie star. Right after Nic filed for divorce from O.J. and moved out, she went to Aspen with Marcello from February to March. That relationship ran into trouble when O.J. called her, screaming that Marcello was bragging all over town that he'd made love with Nicole. She denied it, but O.J. wouldn't believe her. He called Marcello at the salon and threatened him.

It was shortly after this that Nicole had a weekend interlude with Keith—broken up by O.J. The man was still running her love life.

Even while the Marcello relationship was going on, Nicole had not forgotten the young law clerk, Brett Shaves.

"He's cute, but no way," Nic would say, but then she'd smile.

If Marcello hadn't messed things up for himself by bragging about his conquest of Nicole, who knows whether Brett would have ended up sharing Nic's bed. But a bizarre incident occurred on July 16, at a birthday party Nicole threw for CiCi Shahian. Brett was invited, and Marcello was there, but now solely as Nicole's friend. It was a fast-track party, but suddenly we heard the sound of Nicole's nanny, Lisa, screaming in the garage. Nicole and CiCi rushed in and found Marcello roaring drunk with his trousers down around his ankles.

Nicole threw him out and never spoke to him again. That very night Nicole and Brett finally became lovers. The next day, I could hardly wait to get Nic on the phone for details. She was elated but feeling a little uneasy about the age difference.

"Men do it all the time—why can't we?" I asked Nicole.

Nic laughed, "I guess so. He's really nice."

"I just hope the law firm doesn't put his time on O.J.'s bill." We both started laughing hysterically.

On October 15, Nicole's divorce from O.J. was final. About ten days later, she took off for Mexico to celebrate with Brett and Keith, who brought along a girlfriend. Nicole stayed at the seaside resort town of Cabo San Lucas in the same condo she and O.J. had rented when they vacationed there.

That same month I left the home Christian and I had shared together. We just couldn't seem to get it together. I moved into a fabulous gated community on Park Place, next door to California Governor Pete Wilson and just above Vidal Sassoon. Then I started dating Albert Gersten, an entrepreneur who had just opened up a club called The Gate.

One night Albert and I jetted off to Las Vegas to see the Holyfield-Bowe fight. After the fight we phoned Nic in Cabo San Lucas to see how she and Brett were doing.

There was trouble in paradise. Nic said Brett didn't seem to be able to handle their relationship. He was possessive and jealous. She said she had to keep reminding herself that he was only twenty-three years old. He was also intimidated by the fact that O.J. had been in her life and that was starting to bother her.

"I see the handwriting on the wall, Faye," she told me. "I don't want another obsessive or destructive relationship."

Nicole didn't end it with Brett. When she got back to Los Angeles, we fell into our routine of coffee at Starbucks, lunches and dinners at Toscana and Rosti's, then out for a few dances at Roxbury or Bar One or The Gate.

Around Thanksgiving, Albert and I decided to go to Cabo San Lucas with a few people. I asked Nic if she'd like to come, but she had Thanksgiving plans with her children and parents. So did Kris and Bruce. We went with my daughter, Francesca; Albert's daughter; his mother; his aunt; a chef; and a couple of housemen from his Los Angeles home.

When I first laid eyes on Albert's 22,000-square-foot villa in Petra DuGal, which is the "American" part of Cabo San Lucas, I was awe-struck. What a magnificent time that was. So romantic. Every night Albert would order a masseuse for each of us. We'd walk into the gigantic bathroom that overlooked the Pacific Ocean where the centerpiece was a huge Roman tub.

The room was lit by candles and next to the tub was iced champagne set in silver buckets. We'd have our massages while a piano player Albert hired for the occasion played romantic melodies in the foyer. Afterward, dinner would be served in the main dining room by the white-jacketed housemen.

When we got back to Los Angeles, all the girlfriends met at Toscana and then went dancing: Nic, Cora, CiCi, Kris, and I. We were having a great time drinking tequila and dancing with each other. After a while a guy walked up and asked if he could dance with us. I think it was CiCi who looked at him and said, "Ask her," pointing to Nic. The guy looked at Nic then asked "Who is she, the boss?" After that we often called Nic "The Boss" when we went out. The nickname stuck because it summed up what she was becoming, slowly but surely—boss of her own life.

The inner circle was excited. Albert had spent a small fortune on the new club he was about to open in Los Angeles. The opening night was for celebrities and VIPs only. I invited Nicole and Brett; Cora and Ron Fishman; Kris and Bruce Jenner; Kathy and Michel Harouche; YuJu and Ray Evans; CiCi Shahian; my ex-husband, Paul Resnick, a few of the people I loved.

That evening Albert sent a limousine to pick me up and bring me to the new club. He'd been there all day taking care of last-minute details. I had the driver take me to CiCi's home. As she walked to the limo, I was knocked out by the amazing outfit she had on.

"Wow, girl," I said. "You look like a million dollars."

As we pulled up to The Gate I was amazed at the crowds milling around watching the celebrities arrive. CiCi and I were whisked inside and taken to the best seats in the house. I had made careful plans about where my best friends would be sitting, and Albert had everything arranged. There was a VIP section on the upper level, where champagne was flowing like water. The sound system was perfect, and the club was decorated in magnificent detail. The decor was hand-finished and hand-painted. I knew how much work had gone into it.

It reminded me of the care I'd taken finishing the house I had built with Paul Resnick in Beverly Hills. It was Disney Chairman Michael Eisner's former place, and I'd put $1,300,000 into renovation and decoration. What a job that had been. My designer, the famed Warren Sheets, had literally lived and traveled with me for more than a year to research my lifestyle and what I'd need to design a home unique to me. I used to joke that Warren knew more of my most intimate secrets than my husband. Actually, it wasn't a joke.

The Gate opening stands out as one of the best get-togethers we ever had. Nicole and Brett were in a great mood, very loving. All the women danced up a storm, and Albert was the perfect host. The Gate was a grand success!

Sadly, Albert and I broke up shortly afterwards. It was a fine romance, but after a while we both discovered something; he missed his ex-girlfriend, Camille, and I missed Christian. This was just before Christmas. I called Christian to tell him I just couldn't seem to get him out of my system. We agreed to meet over the holidays and talk about straightening out our problems.

Let me flash forward for one last story about The Gate. It wasn't funny then, but I can laugh about it now. After I split up with Albert, I still loved going to his club. It was the best place in town to dance, and Nicole and I loved playing there.

One evening, Nic called me up and said, "Let's go dancing."

'"Nic, I have my ripped jeans on and my hair back in a ponytail."

Nic said, "Oh, just throw on a baseball cap and let's go."

I agreed, and we met at Café Maurice. The

music was loud, the food was inexpensive. Then we went over to dance at The Gate. I looked like some little rapper chick from Melrose in my outfit, but it was fun because I was so comfortable. People stared at me, and Nic and I laughed about it.

A few days later, Nicole and I went back to The Gate again. This time I looked a bit different. I was wearing a black designer dress with open-cut shoulders. We all sashayed onto the dance floor and got into it. We hadn't been dancing five minutes before the head of security came over and said, "Faye, I need to talk to you."

I knew him, of course, because of my association with Albert. "What is it?" I asked.

He said, "I'm going to have to ask you to leave." I was stunned. "Ask me to leave? What are you talking about? I have never been asked to leave anywhere in my entire life!"

"Faye, Camille just can't handle your being here. She gives Albert a bad time whenever you show up. He's gone through hell. So what it comes down to is, Camille doesn't want you back here."

He shrugged apologetically. I realized there was no sense in getting angry with him. The fact was, Nicole, CiCi, and I were being 86-ed. The first place we've ever been kicked out of! Nicole went outside to get her Ferrari. I picked up two long-stemmed roses some men we knew had bought for us. I walked past Albert and Camille. Albert looked like he wanted to disappear.

I smiled graciously and put the two roses down in front of them. "Here's my parting gift to the King and Queen of Disco. Enjoy your club. Bye-bye." And I left.

God, that bothered me. I hated the idea of being kicked out. But I finally calmed down when I re-membered something Sophia Loren had once said to Nicole, "The party doesn't begin until I've ar-rived." I repeated it to Nic and CiCi and we started laughing.

Nic said, "Well, now we're leaving...so I guess the party's over, babe."

* * *

Just after Christmas, Nicole called me up and said, "Would you believe it? Brett's snowed in up at Tahoe. He was supposed to be back today, but it looks like he won't make it in. He says it's awful up there. Do you want to go out tonight and maybe have dinner?'

"Okay, Nic, but I think I'll just hold it to dinner. No dancing for this girl tonight. I've got some shopping I've got to do before New Year's."

"How about Toscana's. See you there at eight?"

We went out and had dinner, just the two of us. Nic was restless again: problems with Brett. We chatted for a while after dinner, some friends joined us for a bit, and then we went home.

I was getting ready for bed when the phone rang. It was Nic. "That little son of a bitch is up in Tahoe with a girl."

"What? How do you know?"

"I called his room at the hotel, and a girl answered. A real drowsy voice. Like I had just woken her up."

"Oh my God, what did you say?"

"I asked her what the hell she was doing in Brett's room, and she said she was just a friend. Some friend. I can't believe I fell for this snowed-in crap."

I let Nic vent for a while. She put me on hold for another call then clicked back.

"It's Brett. You want to hold? This won't take long."

She put me on hold. I waited, thinking of the brutal tongue-lashing young Brett was getting. When Nic was this pissed it was short, cold, and deadly. In less than two minutes she was back.

"Can you believe the nerve of him. He's still sticking to his snowed-in bullshit and says the girl's there because the hotel ran out of rooms and no one can get out."

"Well, Nic, it's possible they are snowed in. You can call the hotel and ask."

"I don't give a good goddamn. If they're snowed in, let that bitch sleep in a snowbank."

I started laughing so hard, I couldn't stop. Finally Nic joined in. After a while I said. "Hey, Nic, why don't we go get snowed in. Let's go to Aspen for New Year's."

"Can we get a room this late?"

"I know a terrific guy, and he's got a great house. Why don't we head for the mountains and have some fun?"

Chapter 7

KATO

*N*icole and I landed in Aspen ready to party. And there were parties a-plenty. The prospect of spending the holiday in Los Angeles was just too boring, so we house-guested with Jerry Ginsberg, a great guy and a friend of Nicole's for many years.

The night we flew in we were whisked to a party for about 500 people at the Ritz Carlton. For entertainment, they had a runway fashion show. Nicole and I were among volunteers who'd been asked to help out by modeling expensive, fancy motorcycle jackets.

Donald Trump was there, doing his "look-at-me, I'm-bigger-than-life" thing. We were all laughing because he'd dragged along this incredibly big-busted bimbo who apparently thought runway modeling was akin to bumping and grinding in a strip show. Her antics were hysterical, but Donald was salivating.

After the show, we went to the lobby area. There were two men standing outside. Nicole said to me of one of them, "Oh, my God, Faye. That man is really beautiful! And he's following me!

"Where is he? I asked. Nicole pointed him out. She was right; this guy was truly gorgeous. He finally approached us and introduced himself as Grant Kramer, an actor.

Grant blew our minds when he claimed that his mother was Terry Moore and his father was Howard Hughes. He was a serious guy, very nice, and he had a pal with him that night, Kato Kaelin.

Kato was a would-be comedian. I remember Nicole and I standing there laughing at his non-stop quips. They weren't all brilliant, but they came at you so fast you never had a chance to stop laughing. But Kato was no sexpot, and when he asked if we wanted to go to the Caribou Club, we took a rain check for the next night. Nicole gave Grant a subtle signal to lose Kato and stay with her. She had designs on him.

Kato finally left the Ritz Carlton with somebody else. Grant came home with us to Jerry's house.

We sat around talking for hours and had a really nice time. Grant stayed over at Jerry's that night, and Kato was apparently somewhere with friends.

After Nicole died, there were reports that she and Kato were lovers. This is absolutely not true. Nicole never had eyes for Kato. He was sweet but had minimal sex appeal. Yet he was so "touchy, touchy"—the kind who was always hugging you or squeezing you or holding your hand—that a casual observer might have assumed something was happening. Ignore those reports and the photos taken of us that night at the Ritz Carlton. Nicole and Kato were pals only.

But Grant...Nicole was absolutely crazy about Grant. He was more serious, and he wasn't as "touchy." Even though he stayed over with us that night at the house, nothing went on. Nicole and I were sharing a bedroom because there was no more space in Jerry's house, and Grant stayed in our bedroom.

When I say nothing went on, Nicole and Grant were kissing and doing some gentle groping, but nothing serious. The three of us stayed up most of the night talking. Grant loved to talk and was fascinated by Nicole. He kept asking intense questions, pushing Nicole to reveal her inner self. Nic kept her cool as usual, but her eyes sparkled. She really liked this guy, and I knew it was going to happen, but not that night.

For the next four days we skied, wined, dined, and hit all the hot spots. At the Caribou Club, we had dinner with Phil Pitzer, Vanna White, and her husband, George Santo Pietro. Grant was with us, and Kato Kaelin tagged along often, although he was always splitting to do his comedy thing with friends. Nothing sexual had happened with Grant and Nicole, but she really dug him. I had little doubt that when we got back to Los Angeles the romance was going to blossom. This handsome man had a really intense side to him, and that appealed to Nicole. He took her very seriously.

Grant and Nicole had a lot of deep conversations while I was with them. He was interested in the whole story of her marriage to O.J. and why they had broken up. Grant was fascinated when he learned that Nicole had been with O.J. ever since she'd come out of high school. O.J. was the person, she told Grant, who had "molded" her, made her into the woman he saw. Grant's response to this was, "Nobody can mold you." Nicole knew better. She told Grant, "I'm a product of O.J., plain and simple."

Nicole truly felt she didn't have her own personality. But she was eager for change, to become "herself." And Grant was just the guy to confide in, to seek advice from.

Grant kept talking about some intensive group therapy sessions he attended in Los Angeles. As we talked together, he said, "Look, I've got secrets to share; you've got secrets to share. Let's go into this group therapy together. It's run by a man named Carl, and it's very heavy, very intensive."

"That really sounds great to me," said Nicole, "I'd like to do that." It appealed to me too. I'd undergone intensive group therapy when I was in the Betty Ford Clinic and I believed it had helped me.

When Grant wasn't talking to Nicole, he loved talking to me about Nicole. He wanted to understand her psyche. I told him she was a beautiful woman with a kind spirit and that what she said about O.J. molding her was absolutely correct. She hadn't formed her own personality and didn't know where she stood in life. What's more, she had just too much pain she was suppressing to let anybody know her.

When we got back to Los Angeles, Nicole and Grant were closer than ever. We actually started going to the group therapy sessions. As time passed, Nicole and Grant continued their friendship. Finally she told me, "Faye, I'm crazy about Grant. I'm going to "do" him."

I laughed. "Have fun, Nic!" I said. "And I *know* you will!"

I couldn't wait to hear Nic's report on her first sexual encounter with Grant the morning after. Girls will be girls, after all. But Nicole was not all bubbly and excited. In fact, she sounded a little bit disappointed.

At first she didn't want to talk about it, but I finally drew her out. Part of the problem was simply the wrong chemistry. The other part was that Nic was a very powerful woman, sexually. When she and O.J. were together, they had sex up to five times a day. In fact, when Nicole and O.J. were divorced, Nic often talked about the problem of not having enough sex. She really liked sex with O.J., and Nic had strong appetites. Grant, apparently, was no O.J.

But she still liked Grant. She found him sensitive and responsive to her emotional needs. One thing that struck me as odd was that Grant could never hear enough about her sex life with O.J. He appeared fascinated with O.J.'s sexual prowess, his lovemaking techniques, and Nicole's voracious appetites.

* * *

Kato Kaelin suddenly appeared on the scene, wisecracking and playing the court jester. Kato had no place to live and was trying to put together, with no visible success, an agency for movie and TV extras. Kato began to offer to baby-sit for Nicole's kids, and she let him move into the guest house behind the Gretna Green house, rent free.

It was a perfect arrangement for both of them, Kato was not only great fun, but he loved children. He played games with them incessantly and made Justin and Sydney laugh. Nic was delighted. Watching Kato with the kids, I couldn't help contrasting his actions with O.J.'s stiff, distant behavior with his children. O.J. was one of the world's most renowned sportsmen, yet he almost never played football, catch, or any other sports with his own children.

* * *

O.J. had never liked the idea of Kato living at Gretna Greene. Later, when Nicole moved to the Bundy Drive condo, and there was no separate guest house, she told Kato he could live in a spare room and continue doing baby-sitting and chores. O.J. strongly disapproved. Even though there was nothing going on between Nicole and Kato, O.J.

just couldn't believe that a man and a woman could live in the same house and not have sex. Besides, he didn't like the fact that Nicole would have a male friend around to constantly lean on and ask for advice.

So O.J. lured Kato away from Nicole by offering to let him live in the guest house at the Rockingham estate in exchange for acting as caretaker. When Kato accepted this arrangement and moved to O.J.'s, Nicole was furious. She considered it a betrayal, and she never spoke to Kato Kaelin again.

Chapter 8

RECONCILIATION

*A*pril, 1993. When we love someone we want to believe them. When we're having trouble, we want to believe that things can be different and things can change.

One Sunday morning I had a call from Candace Garvey, Steve's wife. "Hi, Faye. I just saw Nicole at church and she's all excited."

"Why is that, Candace?" I asked her.

"Well, Steve and I and Kris and Bruce Jenner were out of town at a Pro-Am golf tournament last weekend, and O.J. was there with his girlfriend, Paula Barbieri. We're talking with O.J., and he suddenly tells us that he will never cheat on a woman again. He says he's with Paula now and he never wants to womanize again. Isn't that just incredible?"

"Well, we'll see, won't we. "We hung up.

Just then, Nicole called to tell me the same thing

"Oh, my God," she said. "Maybe he's changed. Maybe we could have a sane relationship. Maybe that obsessive behavior of his would stop."

I laughed. "Oh, c'mon, Nicole. A leopard is going to change his spots?"

* * *

I've asked myself this question over and over: Why did Nicole suddenly want to reconcile with O.J. after the divorce? After O.J. realized Nicole wasn't coming back to him, he decided to have nothing to do with her. And he seemed genuinely happy with Paula Barbieri. For once, O.J. was leaving Nicole strictly alone. He refused to speak with her unless absolutely necessary. It made Nicole crazy.

After Nicole, Grant Kramer and I had our intensive group therapy sessions. Nicole achieved new maturity. And hearing from Candace that O.J. had seemingly embraced monogamy gave Nicole the idea that perhaps divorce had caused spiritual growth for both of them.

One morning she phoned me and said, "I'm going to go and put my family back together. I'm going to ask O.J. if he's interested in trying again."

She got into her Jeep and drove over to his house. O.J.'s response was, "Oh my God. This is just too much. I'm happy with Paula. I may not be in love with Paula, but she's good to me. She doesn't hate showing up with me at parties or personal appearances."

Nicole left the Rockingham estate and called me from her car phone. "Well, he's not responding," she admitted. "But I feel good about making the attempt."

About a half-hour later, Nicole phoned again. "Guess what? Guess who just left the house? O.J.—he wants to talk about this whole thing. He likes the idea."

Nicole was bubbling with happiness. She said she'd told O.J., "Let's just take it slow. We don't have to rush and get into any problems over this. Let's just go nice and easy. We've got nothing but time."

He started calling her five or six times that day. It was typical O.J. behavior. Once he got his teeth into something, he never let go until he'd gotten what he wanted.

* * * *

Nicole and I had made plans to fly down to Cabo San Lucas for Mother's Day. We'd take the children and stay at my villa. O.J. and Nicole were working on their reconciliation. Nicole said, "O.J.'s probably going to Cabo for a golf tournament at Palmilla. Do you mind if he stops by and spends a night or so with us?" Nicole wanted the reconciliation to work and I was willing to do anything to help her.

O.J. did join us and stayed for five days. Cabo was wonderful as usual. We'd go jet-skiing, snorkeling, ride horses on the beach, or just hang out by the pool. At night, we'd go to the Giggling Marlin, or we'd play volleyball with the kids on the lighted court at Carlos and Charlie's.

One thing that struck me was that O.J. actually played with the children throughout his stay. It's the first time I ever saw him act like a real dad. It could have been an idyllic time, but the reconciliation turned rocky because O.J. started laying down ground rules.

It bothered O.J. that Nicole had seen other men during their separation and divorce. He'd say, "Things are going to be different, Nicole. You've been leading a single life for a year. I don't want you going out dancing anymore without me, and I don't want all these guys hanging out at the house.

And I don't want you spending so much time with your girlfriends. You've got to start thinking of me; I'm the man in your life."

Nicole told him, "Forget it! I'm not going to go back to you under these conditions."

It was during that trip that I became the de facto mediator. O.J. came to me. "Faye," asked, 'why does she get so offensive with me? Why does she get in my face when I'm just trying to work this thing out so we can live a good life together? She just doesn't seem to understand what I'm trying to say to her."

I said, "Wait a minute, O.J. A reconciliation is *two* people resolving their differences. That means that if you've done things in your past that she doesn't like, or if she's done things in her past that you don't like, you've got to figure out a way to get over it and move on. You've just got to find a way to compromise."

Incredibly, O.J. took my advice to heart—at least for the time being. He told Nicole that he'd try to forget about the men. What's more, he wanted her to understand that he truly wanted to stay faithful to her.

Nicole was thrilled. They became very loving and kind to each other. It ended up being a wonderful trip. Either Cabo San Lucas had worked some magic—or I had. What a special gift for Nicole on Mother's Day.

We flew back to Los Angeles. O.J. took Nicole to dinner at Giorgio's, a chic Santa Monica Italian restaurant. Once there he demanded confessions about the men in her life.

Nicole, predictably, recoiled. She told O.J., "Oh, no...can't we just get on with fixing our relationship without dredging up the past? All I see are red flags here, O.J. We're going to get in trouble."

O.J. was relentless. He said it was absolutely necessary to hear it all. Nicole kept protesting that divulging intimate details of her sex life could be very harmful. But O.J., as always, won.

He made her recite the list of men. She started with Brett, whom she'd been with for six months. She mentioned Marcello. She told him about Joseph, then about her relationship with Grant Kramer. O.J. kept getting hotter and hotter as she went down her list.

Then she came to the one name she desperately didn't want to reveal—but finally Nicole admitted to her affair with Marcus Allen, O.J.'s second-best friend after Al "A.C." Cowlings. She quickly told O.J. that she'd only let him "play" with her; she didn't admit to actual intercourse.

Nicole told me O.J. exploded. He turned on her like a man possessed. He threatened her, saying "If you're ever with Marcus again, I'll...I don't know what I'll do, but it will be real bad. I won't be able to control myself."

He wouldn't let it end. It held up the reconciliation attempt for months. At times we were worried that O.J. might take revenge on Marcus by telling his fiancée, Kathryn, about the affair with Nicole. That would have been a disaster. Kathryn was a sweet woman who was well aware of Marcus's womanizing, but she might have felt she had to call off the wedding. O.J. didn't tell Kathryn, but he did confront Marcus.

No one knows exactly what was said. But it ended with Marcus swearing to O.J. that he would never touch Nicole again. he said it wouldn't be a problem anymore because he was getting married.

All summer long Nicole and O.J. tried to get the relationship going again. But every time they'd have a fight over the slightest thing, O.J. would bring up Marcus.

* * *

It was a long, hot summer. I went out a lot with Nicole and O.J., and I witnessed some of his blowups. The worst was that frightening night at Redondo Beach when O.J. exploded just because Nicole had mentioned Joseph's name.

O.J.'s tempers were truly terrifying. Nicole said he was doing a lot of cocaine. He was certainly drinking heavily.

I kept thinking about Nicole. I felt like I was witnessing the prelude to an impending train wreck.

To understand why O.J. was so compulsively attracted to Nicole, you'd have to understand his mind-set. O.J. seemed to hate being black and, although he tried to conceal it, avoided any real connection with the black community. His marriage to Marguerite was in the days before he knew he could actually cross over the line and, except for the color of his skin, seemingly become white. Marguerite was probably the last black women O.J. would ever be with. Nicole was, in O.J.'s words, "angel white."

Nicole, on the other hand, was virtually color blind. She judged people on the basis of what mattered to her—loyalty, kindness, and concern for others. Nicole even told me how disturbed she was by O.J.'s attitude toward other blacks. She felt that he was in a unique position to help others and that while he was content to be a role model for young black athletes, he never went out of his way to help them. Other black celebrities—Bill Cosby, Sidney Poitier, Whitney Houston, Arsenio Hall, and Oprah Winfrey among them—have given millions of dollars and endless hours to supporting black causes. Their contributions to the United Negro College Fund and other organizations will salvage the futures of a whole generation of black youths who are gravely at risk of succumbing to drugs, being killed by their peers, or otherwise being lost to society.

Nicole was not the first white woman in O.J.'s life, nor was she the last. Before they met, O.J had made it a point to be seen with as many beautiful women as possible—and it was generally understood that only whites need apply. His flirtations and affairs while he was married to Nicole, as well as during their separation, invariably were with women who, while maybe not "beyond white," definitely were a lighter shade of pale.

Chapter 9

A BETTER-MODEL O.J.

When Nicole was married to O.J., she was strictly a one-man woman. Men would flirt, and Nic would laugh it off. She was never unfaithful, never responded the tiniest bit. But one man did intrigue her.

Who could blame her? He was black and beautiful—one of the most debonair men I have ever met. He was eloquent, articulate, and charming. All that and a football hero, too. Men admired him. Women adored him. And O.J. Simpson called him his best friend, next to A.C. Cowlings.

That's why a romance with this man was taboo. But once Nicole had finalized her divorce and tasted the heady wine of freedom, I knew that she was headed for trouble with L.A. Raiders' star Marcus Allen.

Trouble isn't a big enough word to cover this kind of forbidden relationship. Any woman knows the rule: No matter how tempting, you don't "do" your man's best friend.

Marcus Allen was as close to O.J. Simpson as Al Cowlings. A.C. had a buddy relationship with O.J. that went all the way back to childhood. Marcus was always dependent on O.J., although he was a star in his own right. He had money, independence, and power. Marcus looked up to O.J., admired him, treated him like a mentor.

When Marcus had his highly-publicized differences with Raiders' owner Al Davis, O.J. was right there defending him against the world. Marcus and A.C. were O.J.'s only close black friends. If you looked at most of O.J.'s pals, they were older, affluent, white Jewish men. These were O.J.'s golfing buddies, his country-club pals. But when O.J. hit the town and wanted to howl, when he was looking for women, Marcus was his running mate.

They chased women, and when they caught them they passed them back and forth—O.J. to Marcus, Marcus to A.C.; they *all* eventually got the girl. That was part of the dance. But the real trip was who'd get the girl *first*.

These were athletes, pro-footballers. Winning was everything. Competition never died with them. O.J. was the older man, whose days on the football field were past. Marcus was the up-and-comer, the new star. But O.J. never failed to show Marcus that he still had the fanciest footwork when it came to chasing women. O.J. was the big dog. Marcus beat him just enough to keep the game interesting.

The first time I ever saw Marcus with Nicole, I picked up on the attraction instantly. How O.J. missed it, I'll never know. Marcus was very cool when O.J. was around, of course, and maybe it was just too subtle for a man to pick up on. A woman could see it a mile away. Nicole admitted to me that even during her marriage, Marcus was very seductive when O.J. wasn't around. He tried to talk her into bed more than once, and Nicole never got angry at him for it. She'd just laugh it off, sort of giggle and pretend it wasn't happening.

Marcus was never aggressive with Nicole. He played it casual and easy. But he took his best shot. He'd make the suggestion and watch the response. It was as if he figured that if he kept it on the front burner between them, maybe someday Nicole would go for it if the relationship with O.J. soured. Marcus never got intrusive, never got rude. It just wasn't his style, and he was one of the most stylish men I have ever known.

Marcus just lit Nicole's fire. She told me once, "I like him so much, I just always feel good when he's around."

The first time I met Marcus, I discovered first-hand why Nicole was so impressed. It was at a birthday party for Ron Hardy, manager of the Monkey Bar, at Nicole's house after her divorce.

Marcus was such a gentleman, so smooth, so well spoken. He exuded charm. But after we chatted awhile, he made it very clear that he wanted me. He went so far as to tell Nicole, and she promptly told him "Faye's a very good friend; you'd better be cool, Marcus."

At this point, Nicole and Marcus hadn't begun their affair, and to Marcus I was just fair game, another woman to be tackled. The next week he called Nicole and said, "I want to go to the Monkey Bar, and I'd like you to invite your friend Faye."

I called Kris Jenner. "Kris, I don't know what to think about this. I know Marcus Allen has been trying to get my phone number, and Nicole wants me to go out with them tonight to the Monkey Bar. I like Marcus, but not that way. On the other hand, I'd like to keep him as a friend because he's a friend of Nicole's. What do you think?"

Kris said, "Whatever you do, don't go out with Marcus Allen. He's the biggest womanizer in the world. And don't forget he's engaged to Kathryn. She turns a blind eye to his fooling around, but it hurts her when he does it publicly."

I ended up going to the Monkey Bar that night. A lot of our crowd was there, including Keith Zlomsowitch. Keith ordered Cristal champagne and Beluga caviar for Nic and me. Ron Hardy was there; rock star Don Henley was there. Then Marcus and A.C. came in and joined us.

Marcus sat down. Within moments he put his hand on my thigh under the table. I immediately said, "Marcus, take your hand off of me."

"Why? Aren't you single? Didn't you leave Christian?"

I said, "Yes, I am single, but no, I'm not interested in you. Just take your hand off of me. I'm not one of the women you're going to do this with. You need to understand that."

Marcus was offended. He looked at Nic. "I can't believe what your friend just said."

"I told you last week to be cool with my friend," snapped Nicole. "Why don't you believe me? If you want to be her friend, you can stay. If you don't, Marcus, you'll have to leave."

After Nic and I finished our caviar, Marcus and

A.C. suggested we go out dancing at Bar One or Tatou. I didn't want to go because I knew what was going to happen. I'd slowed Marcus down, but I knew I hadn't stopped him. So I said, "I'd rather not, Nic. If you want to, go ahead."

Nic said she'd stay. So Marcus and A.C. left after we told them we might join them. Nic and I ended up sitting there and having a long conversation. That's when she confessed, "Faye, I really have a crush on Marcus."

"That's great, Nic. But don't you think that's a little volatile? This is O.J.'s closest friend after A.C. And divorce or no divorce, you know how O.J. feels. If I were you, I'd stay as far away from Marcus as possible. You're playing with fire."

Nicole shook her head impatiently. "Marcus is very discreet. He knows that O.J. would get crazy, so he'd never let anybody know about us. It would be okay."

"I disagree with you, Nicole. Marcus is cute, really neat—and all that other stuff. But you're going to get burned."

Nicole let her hair down that night. I thought, *My God, she's really crazy about him.* She told me about all the times he'd tried to talk her into an affair. Because she was married, she hadn't done anything with him. But now that she was divorced, she said she was actually considering it.

"I think you're asking for trouble," I told her. All I could think about was how O.J. would react if Marcus ever touched Nicole. Sure, he and Marcus passed women back and forth. But it was unacceptable to O.J. for anybody to even look at Nic. Although she was his ex-wife, he still treated her like his possession. Nobody touched Nicole.

I had an uneasy feeling about this, and I just couldn't shake it.

Then Keith came over to our table. He wanted us to join the owner of the Monkey Bar, Jack Nicholson's best friend, Alan Finkelstein, who was sitting with Don Henley. Nicole, and I had never met Don before, so we went over to their table and had a great time. Don was with his girlfriend, Sharon, a successful model and a very nice girl. After a while, Don suggested, "Why don't we all go over to my house?" Sharon echoed him, saying, "C'mon, you guys. Let's go!"

Keith said, "I'd rather you guys come with Ron and me. We can all go out."

Now I got the picture. Keith and Ron had their own designs on us. We told Keith we wanted to go with Don. So we all caravanned to Don's house on

Mulholland Drive—Don and Sharon leading in his black Porsche, me at the wheel of Keith's Lincoln because he was too drunk to drive, and Nicole bringing up the rear in her Ferrari.

It was a great night. Don had an incredible home and gave us the guided tour. We played music and talked until about six o'clock in the morning, when Nicole said, "I have to go home; the kids are going to be waking up soon."

* * *

Not long after our night at Don Henley's, Nicole phoned me and said, "You remember what I was talking to you about...about Marcus? He just left my house."

I said, "Really? Oh God. Where is O.J.?"

"O.J.'s out of town."

"You're nuts. You really are nuts."

"Well I didn't do anything with him."

"Nic, you're setting yourself up."

"Well, I just want to keep him as my friend."

I knew Nic was hiding what had really happened. She was dying to talk to me about it, but she wasn't ready to admit everything. She knew I didn't approve and that bothered her.

Over the next few weeks, at least eight or nine times I would sense she was being reticent, speaking in a guarded way like someone was with her. I would say, "Nic, is Marcus there?" And she would say, "No." I would say, "Well, I'm on my way over, Nic. I want to sit out by the pool with you." Then she'd quickly say, "Oh, Faye, I'm just going out the door...I've got to pick up the kids." Then I'd say, "Nic, the kids don't need to be picked up until three o'clock this afternoon. What are you doing?"

Nic was the type of woman who loved having her best friends pop in at her house. Some people hate for you to drop in without calling first. But Nic was always delighted at being surprised by a visitor—which always amazed me because I can't stand anyone showing up unannounced. I kept catching her in these evasions, and finally I said, "Nic, this doesn't make sense. Before you wanted me to come over every chance I got. Now, you're keeping me away. What's happening?"

Nic finally confessed. "I'm having an affair with him, Faye."

Silence. I couldn't speak. I had to catch my breath before I could respond, "Nicole..."

"Faye, don't make me feel bad about this. I know you can't understand it. But I've been over this a million times in my head. I mean, why can't I see who I want to see? I'm not married to O.J., dammit. Marcus is not only a good friend, he makes me feel good. You know what I mean? And anyway, O.J. hasn't even been talking to me lately. Unless I have something to tell him about the kids, he doesn't even take my calls. And he's telling everyone how happy he is with Paula Barbieri. So I don't think I'm doing anything wrong."

God, she was right. When you looked at it that way, logic was on Nic's side. A divorce doesn't cut every emotional tie with the stroke of a pen. Still, to me, Marcus was taboo. You just don't "do" the best friend of a guy who still considers you part of your life.

And what the hell was going through Marcus's head? Maybe men are different. How could you be O.J.'s best friend, yet sneak around behind his back and commit a seduction you knew damn well was going to infuriate him?

I knew I had to say something. But Nic was braced to fight me. I already told her my feelings, so I just said, "Nicole, you're my dearest friend. I love you. And I'm not trying to judge you, it's just that I'm worried."

* * *

Nicole's affair with Marcus made me think of a comment A.C. once made: He said Nicole was ruined by O.J. because she would never be able to be with a white man, ever. From many conversations I had with Nicole, I knew she was almost at the point where she believed she had to be with a black man. Color, per se, meant nothing to Nicole. She loved people, and I never heard her make a comment about any race or group that could be considered prejudiced.

But we all have preferences. Men, in general, turn women on—and vice versa. But there are specific characteristics that attract us—body type, hair color, color of eyes, intellect, strength, etc. Some gentlemen prefer blondes. Others like women with big breasts. Some men actually prefer smaller-breasted women. A lot of women like a nice tight behind on a man. And there are women who frankly prefer a well-endowed man. To others, it doesn't matter.

The truth was that the two men who had truly satisfied her in bed were O.J. Simpson and Marcus Allen. Because of them, Nicole was becoming convinced that only a black man could really satisfy her.

It was an inside joke that O.J. would never lose Nicole because she would never find another man who could give her the quantity and quality she was used to.

When I confronted her about it, she said, "They

weren't the first men in my life, but what the others had was like a mini-pickle or a gherkin compared to what I'm used to. There are exceptions—Joseph and Brett were fine—but it's a gamble. We'll have to see what comes along. A.C. was always saying that O.J. had molded me sexually so that nobody else could ever take his place. Let's hope he was wrong."

Some people might think that other men would be intimidated at the thought of being with a woman who had been with O.J.—that they would feel highly inadequate. But that wasn't the case. Every time she turned around, another man was hitting on Nicole.

Nicole had confided that almost every white man she'd been with didn't satisfy her, didn't measure up. I once said to her, "You know, if I were a white guy, I wouldn't have the *nerve* to expose myself to you."

Nicole laughed, just the way she'd laughed one day around Easter time when we were walking along the beach in Laguna with CiCi. Nicole stopped suddenly, bent down and picked up a chunk of driftwood. She held it out in front of her and said, "This is Marcus Allen."

I guess I looked puzzled for a moment. With a

sly smile she said, "This is the size of Marcus Allen."

I said, "Oh my God, that's impossible." The three of us started laughing so hard we couldn't stop. Later, when Nic and I were alone, I asked her, "Nic, were you kidding about that driftwood. Is it really true?"

"It's absolutely the truth," she told me.

For months afterward, every time we wanted to get a rise out of Nic, we'd just say "driftwood!"

Chapter 10

THE MANIPULATOR

BEVERLY HILLS, CALIFORNIA
1994

*T*he reconciliation lurched forward. On again, off again. One minute it was okay. The next it was O.J. screaming about Marcus or some other man Nicole had seen during their time apart. And when O.J. actually spotted one of these men in public, there was hell to pay.

One night, O.J., Nicole, CiCi, Cora, Christian, and I were at Toscana for dinner. Our waiter was the fabulous Marco, the man Nicole liked so much, and who was fated to become her seventh pall-bearer. O.J. had positioned himself, as he always did, facing the door so he could see who was coming in and out. He was the world's biggest gossip. He loved to observe people and their foibles so he could talk about them later. We always teased O.J. about sitting in the "view" seat.

That night my back was to the door. Someone came in the restaurant, but I didn't bother to turn around. I saw O.J.'s eyes squint and a nasty light came into them.

"What's going on?" I asked him.

"Don't turn around, Faye," he ordered, "and do not acknowledge the presence of this person who's just walked in. I know he's your friend, and I can't handle that. I will not have you talking to him."

I asked, "Well, who is it?"

"It's Marcello," said Nicole.

O.J.'s eyes were unfocused. Beads of sweat popped out on his forehead. When I saw that, I knew better than to defy him and turn around. What really annoyed me was that Christian, who had been a friend of Marcello's forever, didn't dare turn around and acknowledge him—an added irony considering that Marcello was the man who had introduced me to Christian.

I put my hand on O.J.'s arm and said, "O.J. whatever you do, please don't create a scene."

"I can't help it, Faye," he said, barely under control." Can you believe this man coming in here, knowing we're in here?"

"O.J. it's a public place—people do that," I said.

"I'm going to get up and beat the shit out of him. I'm going to..."

I said, "No you're not."

Nicole, sitting on the other side of O.J., put her hand on his arm. He kept shifting in his seat like a bull pawing the earth. O.J. is a powerful, athletic man. This was the first I'd been so close to him when he was gripped by one of his rages, and I could feel the heat of his fury. It struck me how ludicrous it was that two women would even attempt to restrain him. If O.J. suddenly decided to charge Marcello, he'd brush us off like flies.

Nicole and I started patting O.J., squeezing his arms, trying to soothe him, saying, "Be cool... don't do it...he'll leave pretty soon..."

When it looked like he'd calmed down, I said, "'I'll be right back. I'm going to the ladies' room. Christian, why don't you move into my seat?"

Marcello was at a table on the way to the rest rooms. As I walked by, I whispered without looking at him, "Marcello, if I were you, I'd leave. O.J. wants to beat you up. Get out of here."

I learned later that the maître d', a friend of mine, had already said to Marcello, "Why don't you go, Marcello. This is wild!" Marcello got up quickly and left, O.J.'s hate-filled eyes boring into his back.

When I came back from the rest room, I was relieved to see that Marcello had escaped unhurt, but Nicole was angry, exasperated.

We talked the next day over lunch. Nic said, "Faye, believe me, when O.J.'s relaxed and happy, he's the most loving man a woman could ever want. He's sweet, he's kind, and the sex has always been so incredible. But why can't the good times ever last? He makes me feel like everything's going to be so wonderful—then in one instant, everything goes to hell. Why can't he control his temper? Doesn't he know how much it hurts me?"

I sighed and hugged her. I saw the pain coming back into her eyes.

* * *

That summer the word drifted along the Brentwood and Beverly Hills grapevine and into the trendy bars and clubs along Sunset Strip: O.J. had Nicole back again. O.J. wanted the world to know that the woman who'd divorced him now wanted to reconcile.

Now O.J. wanted to show Nicole off, so we were going out a lot at night together. One evening, O.J., Nicole, Christian, and I were at Babylon for dinner and drinks. The bill was incredibly high—about $600 for the four of us. A big chunk of the tab was for margaritas, and most of them were consumed by O.J.

Then we took off for Bar One. Prince was there that night. Gregory Brown, a friend who's a producer for Spike Lee, pointed him out. Prince was sitting in a booth, but you couldn't see him. The booth was entirely blocked by four burly bodyguards standing in front of it.

We were seated, and Christian and I immediately went off to dance. When we came back, we saw that Arsenio Hall was seated next to our table. O.J. and Nicole had joined him. By this time, O.J. was drunk, absolutely wasted. It was embarrassing. Finally, Arsenio said to him quietly, "Hey, O.J., I know you're happy to have your lady back, so don't blow it, man. Don't mess it up now by getting drunk."

Moments later, Gregory Brown came over and told to me, "Faye, you'd better get O.J. out of here before the press sees him like this." We had to half-carry O.J. out of Bar One. He was in bad shape. Ron, the manager, helped the three of us get him to his Testerossa. He couldn't drive, of course, so Nicole got behind the wheel.

A small crowd had gathered outside the club,

and everybody was shouting: "Juice...Juice... Juice!" As Nicole started to drive off, O.J. flung the car door open and suddenly started vomiting, practically on the feet of the bystanders.

Incredible! This man could do no wrong in the eyes of the public. Here he was throwing up, and the fans were still shouting "Juice."

The next day, talking it over, I cheered Nicole up and finally got her laughing by saying, "They should have been chanting "juiced...juiced!"

Happy Fourth of July. The inner circle all showed up at Kris and Bruce's annual barbecue. The day before, as usual, they threw a birthday party for me. It was the usual fun and games.

We left the Jenners in mid-afternoon and drove to Laguna Beach, where O.J. owned a magnificent beach house. The group consisted of CiCi, Cora and Ron, Christian, Nicole's sisters, Dominique and Tanya, O.J., Nicole, me, and all the kids.

I loved that beach house. It was a wood frame on four levels graduating down to the shore. It had several guest rooms and was beautifully decorated. We all strolled down to the beach and hung out. At one point, O.J. said to Tanya, "What are you doing lately, Tanya?"

"Well, I'm trying to raise money to go to college," she answered.

O.J. raised his voice, speaking loudly enough to get everyone's attention: "No problem, Tanya, I'll pay for your tuition. You can get started immediately—now that Nicole and I are back together."

Nicole looked at me and rolled her eyes, as if to say, "There he goes again."

This was typical O.J. manipulation. He'd use his money to help someone, which is a good thing. But O.J. demanded your loyalty if he helped you. And he never helped quietly. He always made a big production out of it, letting people know that he was a generous guy.

Yet, to be fair, O.J. had been very helpful to Nicole's family. He'd assisted Nicole's mother, Juditha, set up her travel business. He put her dad, Lou, into his Hertz dealership. And he'd hired Nicole's cousin to manage his fast-food chicken restaurants in Los Angeles. Now he clearly expected Dominique and Tanya to carry this message back to the family: "As long as Nicole and I are together, it's good times for everybody. But, if we're not..."

That night we all went to one of our favorite restaurants, Los Brisas, right at the beach. Things started out just fine, and we were all feeling mellow. Then O.J. suddenly started ranting and raving against smoking. Some of us girls had just come back from having cigarettes outside, and O.J. started in.

"Why don't all of you stop smoking? It's the worst habit. It's unhealthy, and if you don't care about your own health, think about how you're putting our children's' lives in jeopardy. There's no excuse for smoking."

I was furious. I said, "O.J., why do you feel the need to manipulate everyone around you? Just because you don't smoke cigarettes, you want everybody else to conform to you. You're you—and I'm me. Just leave us alone and we'll live our lives the way we see fit."

It wasn't that I wanted to put a seal of approval on smoking. I just didn't want O.J. Simpson to dictate the personal habits of the world—or me.

Nicole, CiCi, Cora, and I finally got him to stop. We went outside again and left the guys sitting there. O.J. had made us all angry. We vented our annoyance by having yet another cigarette.

Later that night, Christian admitted to me that O.J. started up again on smoking the minute we left. Then Christian told me that he thought O.J. was right. I exploded!

"What kind of a hypocrite are you, buying into O.J.'s bullshit? You smoke sometimes yourself!"

Looking back on it now, that evening was O.J.'s

opening shot in a vicious campaign to poison the inner-circle men against their women. I remember that after we finished dinner at Las Brisas and were having a few drinks, O.J. started in again.

"You know, I'm really getting tired of you girls always going out dancing," he said, turning to the men. "How about you guys?"

I couldn't believe it. Suddenly, Ron and Christian were nodding their heads up and down like trained seals, agreeing with O.J.'s preposterous complaint.

"What business is it of yours, O.J.? We've always gone out dancing," snapped Nicole.

"Yeah, well, I just think you shouldn't be going dancing."

Cora looked at Ron accusingly and said, "Ron, you always encouraged us to go dancing."

I was glaring at Christian, waiting for him to defend our right to enjoy ourselves. When he didn't speak, I said, "Christian, you've always encouraged us to go dancing. Now, all of a sudden, you're caving in and changing your opinion just because it doesn't agree with O.J.'s point of view. What the hell is this?"

After that it was like World War III. The women were furious. I told Nicole afterward, "You know how much I love you, and I know you're just as upset as I am. But I can't be around O.J. if he's going to get into conversations like that. How dare he lecture us? Who does he think he is?"

Nicole sighed. "Believe it or not, he's a lot better now than he was when we were married. Hearing about the men I saw when we were apart made him want to get control of me again. But I think I can handle him better now. I know he's not perfect by a long shot, but you have no idea how much of a change I see in him. I don't know if this reconciliation can work, but I intend to keep trying."

I sensed the meaning behind Nicole's words. She meant that O.J. wasn't beating her. She'd hinted about the abuse she'd suffered during her marriage. And I knew about the 1989 beating that made headlines. But at this point, she'd never told me how badly O.J. had beaten her. That would come later. God, this was all so sad. Nicole had apparently decided that mere verbal abuse was a major improvement.

Over the next few weeks, I started noticing more and more how O.J. was manipulating the guys in the inner circle. He was like a wolf leader gathering his pack to control the enemy—us, the women. We all sensed it and vowed we weren't going to be dominated.

My theory on it all? O.J. had been so demoralized when he lost Nicole for the first time he was now lining up a support group to help him keep her in line.

Here's how O.J.'s plan went: First, he told Nicole not to see guys or have them at the house, even if they were just friends; second, he made her sneak cigarettes, making her feel bad about herself, rather than accept her behavior; third, he told her she couldn't go out dancing with her girlfriends unless he was out of town, or spend too much time with them; fourth, he convinced our men to control their women and keep them home more, thereby effectively isolating Nicole; and fifth, he started trying to control Nicole's family again by throwing them financial rewards.

1994: O.J., Nicole, Faye and Christian Reichardt at O.J.'s New York condo before leaving for the opening of the Harley Davidson Club.

May 1993: Nicole and Faye photographed by O.J. on Mother's Day at Faye's villa.

Nicole's favorite photo of Sydney and Justin, used for her Christmas cards in 1993.

Easter Sunday, April 1994: at the Jenner villa in the Palmillia resort after an
Easter egg hunt on the beach. Back row: Freddy DeMann, Candy DeMann,
Bruce Jenner, Kris Jenner, O.J., Nicole, Faye, Christian Reichardt,
Dominique Brown, a boy friend, Simone Harouche, Kimberly Kardashian.
Front row: Justin Simpson, Kourtney Kardashian, Sydney Simpson,

Left to right: Faye, Simone Harouche, Kimberly Kardashian, Francesca
Resnick, Kourtney Kardashian and Justin at Cabo San Lucas.

August 1994: Justin and the Power Rangers on his sixth birthday, his first birthday without his mom.

Aspen, New Year's Day, 1993: Kato Kaelin, Nicole, Grant Kramer and Faye.

October 16, 1993: Nicole, O.J. and Faye at O.J.'s New York condo.

April 2, 1994: O.J., Nicole, O.J.'s friend, Freddy DeMann and Bruce Jenner.

May 9, 1992: Isha Levy, Nicole, and Joseph Perrulli: Nicole is signaling "Peace" to Faye and Cynthia Shahian.

April 3, 1994: Nicole and Faye at Casa Olson at the Palmillia resort in Mexico.

May 1993: Sydney in the pool at Faye's villa in Cabo San Lucas.

1993: Cora Fishman, Faye, Cynthia Shahian and Nicole at dinner at Toscana in Brentwood.

April 2, 1994: Back row: Dominique Brown and a boy friend, Christian Reichardt, O.J. and Nicole. Front row: Erin Brown, Robert Kardashian, Jr., Francesca Resnick, Sydney, Khloe Kardashian. Faye took this photo after snorkeling at the Palmillia Beach in Cabo San Lucas, one day before O.J. left for Puerto Rico.

October 15, 1993: Faye and Nicole at the Harley Davidson opening. One "O" in "Harleywood" had been punched out by George Foreman.

April 1, 1993: O.J., Nicole, Bruce Jenner, Faye and Christian Reichardt at Casa Olsen in the Palmillia resort.

1992: Brett Shaves, Nicole, and Ron Hardy.

Mother's Day, May 1993: Nicole and O.J. on the first day of their reconciliation in Cabo San Lucas at Faye's villa.

Faye and her daughter Francesca on the beach at Cabo San Lucas.

Faye and Sydney at the Giggling Marlin, Cabo San Lucas.

Chapter 11

HARLEY-DAVIDSON CAFE

New York, New York
October 1993

*B*ack from Europe. I could hardly wait to hear all the news, so I drove over to Nicole's before I even unpacked. Over cappuccino in her kitchen, I asked, "So how's it been going with O.J.?"

"It's on and off," she sighed. "Sometimes it's great. Then I find out he's with Paula. Or he starts complaining about my behavior again."

I looked at her intently. "But he hasn't...you know..."

Nicole shook her head. "No. He knows better."

So the reconciliation still wasn't official. God, it was up and down like a yo-yo. Then the whole world found out about it from a front-page story in the *National Enquirer*.

This was in October, just as Nicole and I were leaving to join O.J. for the grand opening of the Harley-Davidson Café in Manhattan.

He'd also invited Christian, who was to fly in later. Nicole and I were in a limousine on the way to the L.A. airport when the driver told us he had a message from O.J. Nicole was to pick up the *Enquirer* at the airport, so we grabbed a copy and read the story after take-off. We were stunned! The details about the reconciliation were so accurate a member of the inner circle must have leaked them.

I said,"Nicole, all this stuff is coming from someone really close to you. They even use your exact words here."

Nicole was stupefied. "Yeah, somebody's giving them information, somebody really close. It's got to be from the inner circle itself."

The *Enquirer* story mentioned the 1989 battering charge against O.J., the one O.J. screamed about in the famed 911 tape—the one that was played on TV and radio stations after the murders. In that tape, O.J. raged about the oral sex Nicole had performed on Keith Zlomsowitch—and the fact that Joseph Perrulli's number was still on her telephone speed-dialing button. He also kept demanding to know how the *Enquirer* was able to quote her exact words so accurately.

When we arrived in New York, a limo whisked us to O.J.'s luxury condominium on 65th Street. It's a gorgeous place, beautifully decorated in masculine dark wood with huge windows and expensive Persian rugs.

When we arrived, O.J. was the perfect host. It was really cute how he welcomed us in, then dramatically opened up the refrigerator to show Nicole he'd filled it full of Beluga caviar—her favorite food. He'd also bought fresh baked breads, candies, and many other wonderful delicacies for us. When I went into the guest room, I was touched to find that there were fresh flowers there, too.

Whenever I think of O.J. today and reflect on all that has happened, I marvel at how considerate, how charming he *could* be. It's sad to remember that I once loved him as a friend.

The next day, Christian arrived and the boys decided to take us shopping. We went to Barney's, where O.J. bought Nicole some fashionable but casual clothes. Nic and I found some matching cross necklaces. Then we went to Donna Karan's showroom, which was our idea of heaven. We lunched at Le Relais, and that night it was off to the Harley-Davidson Café opening.

I have never seen such a jam-packed event.

There were lines all the way down the block. Even super-models and celebrities were being turned away.

What was great about that night was the way O.J. showed Nicole off. I'd seen him shunt her aside so many times as he grabbed the spotlight for himself. But now he wanted to show her off to the world. Every time he saw a camera, he put his arm around her and grinned proudly as if to say, "Here she is, world—I've got her back!" Nicole had always hated cameras, but on this night, I knew she loved the attention she was getting from O.J.

The next night, Christian had to fly back to California. Nicole, O.J., and I went to dinner at the Harley-Davidson Café with Mark Packer, the owner. At dinner, O.J. shocked me when he suddenly ducked his head down below the level of the table top and sniffed a spoon of cocaine. A strange thing happened then—O.J.'s jaws seemed to lock. He looked like he was clenching his teeth. It was nothing short of bizarre.

Later we went dancing at a very chic club. We were having a good time and moved onto another club. Then O.J. again did something that astounded me. He had always acted as if Christian was a close friend. He went out of his way to treat him like a special person, and Christian acted like

O.J. was a demi-god. But as the evening progressed, O.J. noted that Mark Packer had a crush on me. He said, "You know, Nicole, Christian's really not Faye's type. He could never really provide her with what she needs, or what she's used to. Mark's wealthy and cosmopolitan. He'd be much better for Faye."

Nicole was horrified and angry. "'That's so typical of you, O.J. You pretend to Christian that he's one of your best friends. Then the minute he leaves you try to set Faye up with another man. You're not only disgusting, but you're stupid to think Faye would go for that. You're dealing with the wrong girl."

O.J. immediately backed off. "I was just kidding, Nicole. Why do you flair up at me like that? It was just a joke."

"It's no joke!" she responded coldly.

For once, I didn't open my mouth. I knew that if I said anything, it might be the end of my friendship with O.J. I was so angry. How could he be so disloyal to Christian when Christian was so deeply loyal to him.

Later, Mark's driver picked us up and drove us back to O.J.'s. On the way, Mark kept trying to talk me into stopping off at his place to "play a little backgammon." I wasn't interested in playing any games with Mark and politely let him know that.

Mark's driver dropped him off, then took us on to O.J.'s place. We weren't in the condo more than five minutes when the phone rang. I was in my room, and O.J. and Nicole were in the kitchen. O.J. answered the phone. It was Mark Packer. After chatting with him for a moment, O.J. said, "Yeah, Faye's here. Just a minute." He called me and handed me the phone.

As I spoke with Mark, I could hear Nicole and O.J. fighting in the kitchen. It momentarily distracted me, then I heard Mark say, "I'd like to send my driver over to pick you up."

"I beg your pardon? Mark, I just told you that I wasn't interested in anything but getting some sleep. And that's what I'm going to do right now. Good night."

As I hung up, I heard Nicole yell at O.J.,"Why didn't you just tell him that she was sleeping? What the hell are you trying to do here?"

I just didn't want to get into it. I acted as if I hadn't heard a thing. "Good night," I said and went off to bed. I slept fitfully because they continued fighting for hours. I remember feeling very nervous for Nicole. Every time O.J. got as angry as this, I couldn't stop thinking, *Is he going to start hitting her?*

The next day we got up late and packed for the return trip to Los Angeles. Tension was thick. O.J. and Nic weren't even talking. What had started out as a beautiful trip had turned into a disaster. And all because O.J. couldn't stop manipulating everybody and everything—including *my* love life.

Chapter 12

UNHAPPY HOLIDAYS

BEVERLY HILLS, CALIFORNIA
CHRISTMAS 1993

*M*erry Christmas. On December 23, I went over to O.J.' s place. Nicole and A.C. were there. Sydney and Justin were playing quietly among the unopened presents, and there was a wondrous Christmas atmosphere in the house. It was one of those times when Nicole was really into O.J. It didn't hurt that he'd given her a pair of diamond drop earrings. They were glorious—about two carats per drop, or six carats per earring. Nicole loved them.

All during that evening, O.J. sat in a chair, and Nicole lounged on the floor at his feet, wrapping presents, looking up at him adoringly. *How bewildering*, I thought.

Lately, I never knew what mood I'd find them in. I'd been prepared for stress between them because I knew they'd had a huge blowup just two days before. Nicole had called me fuming about it.

"You won't believe this, Faye! I've been over at O.J.'s all week setting up the tree, and, along with the children decorating it, as well as ordering wreaths and planning the Christmas menu. Then guess what's delivered to the house—a festive basket of fruit from that damned Paula Barbieri."

"Oh my God, Nic, she must have known you'd be there."

"Of course she did. And she knew I'd be the one to get any Christmas deliveries. It had this lovely little message attached that said, 'Sweetheart, have a lovely Christmas. Sorry we can't be together. Love, Paula.' "

"What a nasty thing to do. She knows you're trying to reconcile, and she sabotages everything. She's just trying to ruin your holidays. What did you say to O.J.?"

"Well, I went in his face, of course—but you know how slick O.J. can be. He claims it's just Paula trying to get even, and he had nothing to do with it. He claims he hasn't been seeing Paula at all, yet she's called the house a couple of times this week."

"So? Are you buying his story?"

Nicole paused. "Well, I'm not sure. He could be telling the truth. He's been awfully nice to me lately, so I'm keeping an open mind. You know how I love Christmas, Faye. I'm really trying to keep us all together."

I had to admire Nic. I don't think I'd have been quite so forgiving. But there she was, sitting at O.J.'s feet just two days later.

The next night was Kris and Bruce's annual Christmas Eve party. O.J. and Nicole said they might not attend. That's why I'd gone over to the Rockingham house the night before so that we could exchange presents. But just before I left for the party, Nicole phoned to say they'd be there for sure. I was so happy. This party was special. Kris always had the house festooned with garlands, wreaths, stockings, Santa Claus and angel fig-urines—and the centerpiece was a professionally-decorated twelve-foot Christmas tree.

I phoned Kris to tell her Nicole was coming after all, but that I was running a bit late. Just about the time I left my house, a calamity occurred at the party: Joseph Perrulli showed up.

Nicole told me later, "God, it was awful. When Joseph walked in, I knew there'd be trouble. O.J. spotted Joseph, and at first I thought it was going to be okay because O.J. walked up to him and said hello. But then O.J. came back looking indignant. He told me we were leaving—immediately."

I drove up to Kris's house just as O.J. came storming out, followed by Nicole, Kris, and a crowd of our friends. I walked up. "What's going on here? Why are you guys leaving?"

Nicole told me, "Joseph showed up. O.J.'s really upset. He caused a scene."

Now he was causing another one outside. Kris was trying to convince O.J. to stay. I said, "O.J., why leave? Why don't you compose yourself? This is Christmas Eve, so let's just enjoy ourselves."

O.J. was adamant. "I won't put myself through this. Kris should have known about this. I think Nicole knew. I feel like I've been set up."

Nicole was standing off to the side, saying, "'I don't understand why this is happening. I'm not doing anything with Joseph. O.J. just gets so upset every time he hears his name."

I was still arguing with O.J. This was terribly sad. I felt tears start when I caught sight of Justin and Sydney, who were also at the party, standing wide-eyed and uncertain behind their mother.

"O.J., nobody knew Joseph would be here," I implored. "It's Christmas, and we shouldn't ruin it for the children. Let's go inside. Please?"

"I won't go for this. I'm leaving...I'm out of here," O.J. barked.

At that, he bundled Nicole and the kids into the car and left. We all stood around for a moment, then went back inside. Despite the momentary damper O.J. had put on the party, we had a good time. Poor Joseph. He was so apologetic. He'd heard O.J. and Nicole weren't coming to the party. He left very early.

About an hour after O.J. had left, he phoned Kris. "Did I leave my jacket there, Kris?"

"O.J., you were wearing your jacket when you left," she told him. "You had it on."

Again, typical O.J. He knew he hadn't left his jacket at the house. He'd called because he just wanted to find out what was going on—if the party had ended because he'd left, and what people were saying about him. I thought of Nicole. Tonight I'd seen the pain return to her eyes. I wondered, *Was the party all over for her?*

* * *

Things got decidedly cooler between Nicole and O.J. after that incident. Nicole asked me, "How can that bastard have the nerve to complain when some guy I'm not even doing anything with shows up at a party—yet it's okay for him to get Christmas baskets with love notes and phone calls from Paula?"

After the New Year, Nicole moved from Gretna Greene to her new $650,000 condominium on Bundy Drive. She was so excited. It was the first and only home that she ever chose on her own. She had a marvelous time decorating it. Kris and I helped her unpack and organize her closets. Then we went out and bought trees and plants at Rolling Green Nursery. Nicole was hopelessly in love with her new home.

Since O.J.'s blowup at the Jenners' Christmas party, it had become clear that Nicole was having serious doubts about the reconciliation attempt. She had actually been planning to move back into O.J.'s Rockingham estate and lease out the Bundy condo as an investment. The real reason she'd needed to buy a place was to avoid capital gains tax from the sale of a condo she had owned in San Francisco. But now that she was beginning to have doubts about O.J., Nicole decided she'd just remain at the Bundy residence before she made a decision.

After the murders, people asked me why Nicole had chosen to live only five minutes away from O.J. if she thought things were turning sour between them. The answer is that she moved to Bundy to be near her friends and the children's school, not O.J. If anything ever convinced me how deeply Nicole loved us all, that decision to be near us proved it.

* * *

Hello Earthquake. Two days after the Bundy move, the infamous 6.8 quake rocked Los Angeles. I called Nicole immediately, knowing she was alone. The kids were in Dana Point with their grandparents. O.J. was in New York. "Are you, okay?" I asked. Nicole's place had sustained damage, and she was freaking out. There were cracks in the walls, and the place was a shambles.

Next day, there were so many aftershocks that Nicole felt she had to be with her children, so I suggested she ask A.C. to follow her down to Dana Point. Nicole said, "Oh, that's a great idea."

A.C. followed her down in his car to make sure she got there safely because the roads were impossible—underpasses were out, signal lights weren't working, and holes had opened up in streets. There was also every chance of another major quake while she was en route.

Meanwhile, Christian's office was a mess, and I helped him get it back into some kind of shape. But I told him, "'I want my daughter out of this town." It was spooky in L.A., scary. "If you want to stay here and treat your patients, that's fine. Francesca will be at Nicole's home in Dana Point."

Christian came with me. That drive down to the Browns' home was unnerving. Nobody was on the road. When we got there, we decided we'd stay with Nicole at night and travel to the office every day. All of his staff was earthquake bound, so we'd get up at five-thirty in the morning, drive into Los Angeles, and try to keep the practice going. At about eight every evening, we'd drive back to spend the night in Dana Point.

Nicole was disturbed about O.J. He felt there was no need for him to go back to California to join his family. He was in Atlanta getting ready for the Super Bowl, and he wanted her there. He'd call and ask, "Nicole, why don't you just leave the kids with Dita and come to Atlanta?" ("Dita" was O.J.'s nickname for Nicole's mother, Juditha.)

Nicole was reluctant to leave the children, with aftershocks occurring constantly. She wanted to go to Mexico and spend some time in Cabo San Lucas with her kids and Francesca to calm everyone down. I couldn't go because I had to help Christian run the office. Most of our staff still hadn't come back after the earthquake. Like so many Angelinos they were tending to their own problems at home.

O.J. hated the Mexico idea and told Nicole

again, "I want you in Atlanta." Finally, Nicole caved in and agreed that the children would be safe with their grandparents. She invited Cora and Ron Fishman and off they went to the Super Bowl. During this period, Ron and Cora attended a lot of celebrity parties with O.J. and Nicole. Cora loved the attention she was getting from some of the big-name men and decided that she didn't want to be in her marriage anymore. When she and Ron returned to Los Angeles, Cora started an affair with a young, black grocery clerk. Nobody knew about it at the time, except Nicole and O.J.

Nicole and O.J. flew to Florida, where he spent $10,000 to hire a yacht for a romantic two-day cruise. O.J. loved that trip so much that when they got back to Los Angeles, he called Christian and said, "I'm going to charter a yacht, and we'll all take an eight-day trip to celebrate Nicole's birthday in May."

When I talked to Nicole, she told me, "No way. I'm not going to spend eight days on a yacht with O.J. If he starts getting weird, there's no way to get away from him and blow off some steam." O.J. was upset when he heard that but Nicole refused to change her mind.

During February and March, we were all agog over Cora's romance. Ron found out about it when

O.J. went to him and said, "Do you know what's happening with your wife?"

Ron was devastated. After the inner circle got over its initial shock, some of us were furious that O.J. would interfere with someone else's marriage. I can't prove it, but to this day I believe that O.J. had hired someone to follow all of us, including Nicole—and that's how he found out about Cora. How else could he have known?

Poor Ron. He was so despondent. It was humiliating for him, a successful doctor who had given Cora everything, only to be replaced by a grocery clerk.

O.J. was as pompous and mean as I've ever seen him. He was literally gloating. He phoned me almost daily, like the busybody gossip he'd always been, saying, "Can you believe that Cora's having an affair?"

I'd say, "Excuse me, you've been having affairs your entire life. What makes it okay for you and not her? Because she's a woman?"

And O.J., the supposed friend who'd told Ron about his wife's infidelity, said piously, "I'm just upset that she's hurting Ron."

Chapter 13

BEVERLY HILLS BREASTS

Beverly Hills, California
The 1990s

Nicole Brown Simpson was a natural beauty: blonde hair; soft hazel eyes; long, shapely legs; well-toned arms. There wasn't an ounce of fat on her lean, perfectly defined muscular frame. She worked out a lot, she swam and jogged. She was a natural athlete, graceful and feline.

In the late seventies, during the pinnacle of O.J.'s NFL football career, thirty-year-old O.J. spotted seventeen-year-old Nicole working as a waitress in Los Angeles. Her innate sensuality was like a magnet to men including O.J. He was one of the fastest cocksmen in town—and he zeroed right in on Nicole.

She was a thoroughbred. Their attraction was instant, and they made wild, passionate love that first night! Within days he'd set her up in her own apartment and bought her a brand new Porsche. Talk about whisking a young girl off her feet! They went together for seven years, then married at his Brentwood estate in 1985. Their marriage was to last for seven years before they divorced. Throughout their nearly two decades together, their sexual attraction to each other was quite astounding.

Sometime late in their marriage, around 1990, O.J. decided he wanted Nic to have larger breasts. And when O.J. made his mind up on something, he was relentless. He tried to persuade her for months. Expanding her bosom was something Nicole did not want to do. Here was a woman, gorgeous and perfectly happy with her body. Yet her husband wanted her to undergo a surgical procedure that would give her silicone implants the rest of her life! Nicole refused repeatedly, but O.J., as usual, got his way.

There are many noted Beverly Hills plastic surgeons—Dr. Richard Ellenbogen, Dr. Frank Kamer, Dr. Steve Hoeflin, and many more. Nicole chose Dr. Harry Glassman, who's sliced and diced some of Hollywood's greatest beauties. Tops in his field, he's also married to actress Victoria Principal.

When it comes to breasts, Dr. Glassman charges more than most. "But then, the best always do!" Nicole told me. The girls in our group used to joke that Harry Glassman's breasts—and those done by his ex-partner, Larry Kopeland—were the only ones worthy of the notoriously expensive LaPerla bra.

Breast implants have come a long way from the Victorian days when glass balls were inserted into women's breasts. And in the 1950s, it was paraffin! Today, breast implants, particularly in Beverly Hills, are almost as common as root canals—and a lot less painful. Almost every woman I know has had breast implants.

Nicole went through the usual six months of adjustment, accompanied by some pain. She was lucky. Some women actually lose sensation around their nipples—she didn't. And from the moment she could stand up and turn sideways in the mirror, she was a very happy lady!

Nicole loved her breasts, and wondered how she ever got along without them. She now believed they were necessary for her body to look proportionate. And she thanked O.J. profusely. Her only reservation was that she didn't like how her breasts looked in clothing. But she thought they were perfect either nude or in a bathing suit.

O.J. loved Nic's new breasts more than she did! But here is the strange part. After Nicole had her breast operation, O.J. then turned the situation around by chiding her constantly. He'd say, "Once the Tittie Fairy comes around, you'd better watch out for your women—because they love their new bodies." O.J. was actually predicting he'd lose her one day!

Two years after her operation, Nicole filed divorce papers. But the breakup was inevitable and had nothing to do with her new bosom.

* * *

In the beginning of my friendship with Nicole, I wondered why she, a woman who enjoyed being a mother so much—and had a beautiful home in which to raise her children—would continually make the conscious choice to avoid having another child.

"Why don't you want more children, Nicole?' I asked, watching with fascination as she assembled the latest Power Ranger toys for her kids. She shrugged. But later that evening at Toscana's, with one too many margaritas under her Kieselstein belt, she told me another of her "little secrets"— the kind of secrets battered women don't like to share for fear of exposing the shame-based mentality that governs their lives.

"O.J. hates me when I'm pregnant. He treats me so badly." She spoke as if she were ashamed.

"Why?" I asked. I couldn't understand. O.J. always made a public appearance of being the proud, doting father-to-be through each of Nic's pregnancies.

"He hates the fact that I get fat,"' she said.

"But all women get fat when they're pregnant," I said incredulously.

"When I was pregnant with Sydney, O.J. went out of his way to make me feel bad about my body. He used it as an excuse to fool around with other women. He found me ugly to look at."

At this moment I felt the kind of compassion only one woman can feel toward another. And I couldn't help recalling my own happy memories of being pregnant with Francesca. I was never happier. For the most part, my husband and his family put me on a pedestal each of those nine months, and I absolutely loved it. I wanted to get pregnant again with my next husband, but he was older, with children of his own, and would never agree. That is the reason I am not with him today.

Now Nicole was telling me O.J. hated her pregnancies. I tried to keep my composure, but my hands started trembling.

"I thought he would change when I became pregnant with Justin," Nic said, "'but he didn't. He continued his affair with Tawny Kitaen...and he would come home and beat me if I confronted him about it."

"Oh, my God, Nic!" I put my arms around her and handed her a napkin as she broke down and cried.

After Nicole told me her "secrets," I felt relieved that I could share my own experience with my second husband, Fadi Halabi. He only abused me once, but it put me in the hospital. Although it was not an abusive relationship, I was too embarrassed to tell anyone about the isolated incident. Why? Because like many battered women, I was made to believe that I was to blame—yet knowing full well that I wasn't.

My reasons for not filing charges were the same as Nicole's. After a man beats you, in many cases what he does next is to "mind-fuck" you into believing that this was a "one-time only loss of control" and that "it will never happen again." In some cases, like mine, it was true. But in Nicole's case, as with most women, it was sadly not true.

Chapter 14

THE FROGMAN COMETH

O.J. wanted us all to go to Mexico for Easter. Nicole and I loved the idea of relaxing in the sun. There was no hint that we were entering the darkest days of our lives.

We flew down to magical Cabo San Lucas and stayed at a fabulous resort called Casa Olsen. The party included Kris and Bruce Jenner and their kids, Nicole's sister Dominique, her boyfriend, O.J., Nicole, me and a bunch of other friends.

It was paradise. We played on the beach or at the pool with the kids. The guys golfed. Later we'd all meet up poolside and order pitchers of margaritas. We'd laugh, talk, get a bit buzzed, then take off for our rooms to change clothes and join up later for dinner, usually at Carlos and Charlie's. The food was fabulous and we'd dance and drink the night away.

What made it a really perfect picture was Nicole and O.J. They were incredibly loving. After all the ups and downs of the reconciliation attempts that had started just about a year ago, I looked at Nicole and began to think, This might really work!

The first day we arrived in Mexico, Nicole and I were sitting alone on the beach while the kids played down by the shoreline. I asked her, "Is everything really okay with you and O.J.? You guys really look like you've worked it all out."

"Faye, I think this is it. We're getting back together for good!" I hugged her and she hugged me back. I was so happy for her.

The very next night, O.J. screwed everything up. We were all at Carlos and Charlie's, and O.J. suddenly started to flirt with a trampy-looking young blonde. He did it openly, enjoying himself hugely, not seeming to care that everyone was watching. I looked at Nicole for a reaction. She looked back at me and Kris, who was sitting with us. Kris and I both said something like, "Can you believe this?" Nicole said nothing. I knew my friend so well. She was blocking, and nobody could block unpleasantness like Nicole. For years, she'd been coping with nightmares far worse than O.J. making a fool of her in public.

Late that night when I was alone, I wondered if I'd just witnessed the end of the reconciliation. Or would Nicole rationalize O.J.'s outrageous behavior by telling herself that a little flirting was okay, as long as the beatings didn't start again. I could imagine her thinking, *I just won't say anything. If I confront him, he'll go nuts again.*

The next day, most of our group hung out down at the beach, snorkeling and playing with the kids. Suddenly, O.J. started telling everybody that Nicole's biggest fear in life is frogs. Most of our friends knew about Nicole's phobia, so strong, so overwhelming, that anyone who knew her well wouldn't even tease her about it. She loathed frogs.

O.J. acted as if it was the biggest joke in the world. He told everybody, "Hey, can you believe this? It's just so ironic that my wife's biggest fear in life is frogs, and I've ended up starring in a TV series called *The Frogmen*!'" O.J. threw back his head and laughed, and looked at us all with his happy, smiling face. That's what made his next words seem so incongruous, so unsettling. "Hey, baby," he jibed at Nicole, "I'm the Frog Man. Now what do you think about that?"

Two minutes later, O.J. got up and left. This time, Nicole wasn't blocking. She turned to me and said, "I don't think that's funny. He finds this to be funny. This is not funny at all. It's cruel. I'm afraid this man will kill me some day." It was one of those shocking statements that are so unbelievable you wonder if you heard right.

The next morning was Easter Sunday. We'd set up an egg hunt for the kids, and they were scrambling all over the beach to find their gaily-painted gifts from the Easter Bunny. Nicole seemed a little distant, but when I brought up the "Frog Man" incident, she shrugged it off, obviously not wanting to discuss it.

The next day, O.J. flew to Puerto Rico for filming on *The Frogmen*. That evening we went to the Palmilla restaurant for dinner . As we sipped cappuccino, Nicole floored me when she said calmly, "That's it. I can't do it. I can't be with O.J. Seriously, it's over."

"Whoa, whoa, lady," I gasped. "You kept telling me for the past three days how much you dig O.J., that everything's bliss, that you're going to move back in together. Then he leaves—and the next minute you tell me you don't want anything to do with him. What the fuck is going on here?"'

I will never forget the look on her face when she repeated her astounding statement of the day before. "I feel that if we get back together, he'll end up killing me. I don't think he's changed."

Nicole looked at me intently. "Remember when I told you about the time O.J. beat me? The time when the police came in 1989?" I nodded. "Faye there were many, *many* other times. I know it's hard to understand, but...I was crazy about that man. You know how connected we were." I nodded again.

"Faye, O.J. totally satisfied me. After we got divorced it was hard for me to adjust to the fact that I wasn't having constant sex. But I never found another man who could turn me on the way O.J. did—except for one." She didn't have to say the name. Marcus Allen.

'But even when we were having all that great sex, O.J. was still getting it on with practically every woman he met. And when I confronted him—when I went in his face and screamed at him about Tawny Kitaen or all those Hawaiian Tropic girls—he'd beat me. Jesus, Faye, that man would hit me hard."

That's when she told me the story that horrified me most. It was early in their marriage. Nicole and

O.J. were staying at one of the fancy hotels on the Strip in Las Vegas and went to a show-biz party. Dean Martin was there, and somehow O.J. decided that Nicole had made him look like a fool in front of Dean.

When they got back to their suite and she was undressing, O.J. started beating her savagely. Nicole was naked, except for a pair of panties, but O.J. grabbed her by the hair, dragged her to the door of the suite, and flung her into the corridor. He went back into the suite and slammed the door, leaving her outside. Naked, beaten, and sobbing her heart out, Nicole lay there curled up in a fetal position for three hours. It was late at night, and the corridor she was in was a private one leading up to the suite, so no one saw her. A security guard making his rounds finally found her.

I was stunned. "Why didn't you ever tell me this before, Nic? It really would have helped me all these times when I was mediating between you and O.J....when I was trying to understand what the hell it is that keeps bringing you back together, then driving you apart."

That night in Mexico, when I asked her how many times she'd been beaten, she answered, "It was a lot, Faye. I can't begin to count the times."

Nicole's worst beating occurred during O.J.'s affair with Tawny Kitaen. "You know how I found out about that, Faye? It was about a year before Justin was born. I was doing some cleaning up at the Brentwood place when I found a jewelry box in O.J.'s dresser. I guess I shouldn't have opened it, but I couldn't resist because my birthday wasn't far away.

"I opened the box, and there was a pair of diamond stud earrings. They were gigantic! I bet they were worth at least $20,000. I was absolutely knocked out. I figured O.J. had bought them for my birthday I could hardly wait! But my birthday came and went—and no earrings. He did give me a gift, but it wasn't those diamond earrings.

"Later, I told a friend the story, and she told me something that made me sick. She said Tawny Kitaen had been showing those earrings off all over town, telling people that O.J. had given them to her. I even saw a picture of her wearing them in a newspaper!

"Do you remember that whole mess, Faye? While O.J. was seeing Tawny, he was cheating on her with others, so I thought she was just another affair. But when I found out about the earrings, it was like I had been kicked in the stomach. I blew up and confronted him. That was one of the worst times. O.J. started beating me, kicking me, punching me. He hit me so hard once I thought I was going blind. He picked me up, took me to a closet, threw me inside, and locked the door. I lay there crying and begging him to let me out.

"After a while I heard the TV go on. And I suddenly realized that sadist was watching a sports show. I don't know how long I lay there, maybe fifteen or twenty minutes. Then I heard him coming toward the closet. He opened the door, and I said, 'O.J., I'm sorry, please let me out. I won't say anything.' He reached down for me, I thought to help me up. But before I was on my knees he hit me again. He punched and kicked me as I crawled farther into the closet. Then he slammed the door and walked away. All I could hear was the TV. I knew he was sitting there, watching that damned sports show again."

After Nicole finished telling me this horrible story, I reached out and hugged her. But the frightening memories kept pouring out, as if something was compelling her, finally, to divulge the whole truth.

'"Faye, that was the worst night of my life. For hours, I don't know how long, O.J. would watch TV, then he'd come back, open the closet door, hit me some more, then lock me up again. I was so scared. I wanted to die. I begged God to help me. I felt as if nobody in the world could help me. I don't know what was worse, the beatings or that awful *fear* of waiting for him to come back and do it again."

All of Nicole's friends thought that she was the strongest woman they'd ever met. Now I knew how strong she'd really been. I was enraged. I told her, "Okay. This is not a game anymore. This is real life. How do we get out of this? What do we do to get you away from this man? I don't want him hurting you ever, ever again."

God, I was furious! How did O.J. get away with this? During her hellish ordeal in that closet, Nicole had felt that "no one in the world could help me." Those words hurt like a knife through my soul. Why didn't anyone help her? This woman had so many friends, a family.

"Jesus, Nicole! What about your parents—and your sisters? I rarely see your sisters around you. What kind of a relationship do you have?" Nicole shrugged. 'We used to be very close. But when I left O.J., they weren't at all supportive. They absolutely wanted me to stay with O.J. It's just like everything else, Faye. O.J. always controls everyone and everything around him.

"Is that possible, Nicole? These are the people you grew up with."

"Faye, you just don't understand. O.J.'s done a lot for my family. They love him. I'm not saying they don't love me. They do. They're wonderful. They just love him more."

Today, when I think of that chilling conversation in Cabo San Lucas, I remember the *National Enquirer* printing a front-page story shortly after Nicole's death reporting that she'd actually made more than thirty calls to 911 to report beatings by O.J. That night in Mexico, when I asked her how many times she'd been beaten, she answered, "It was a lot, Faye. It was too many to count."

Chapter 15

THUMB RINGS

CABO SAN LUCAS, MEXICO
APRIL 5–6, 1994

Next morning I woke up feeling the weight of nightmares that had gripped me. I couldn't remember them, but I knew they'd been triggered by images of those frightening beatings Nicole had told me about.

It was a sun-drenched, perfect Cabo San Lucas day. Nicole and I had decided to take Kris's teen-aged girls, Kourtney and Kimberly along with Simone Harouche, the daughter of one of my best friends, down to the native silver market in the town. (Kourtney and Kimberly are Kris's daughters by her ex-husband, Robert Kardashian, an ex-music industry executive. Today, of course, Robert is widely known as the O.J. confidant who took up his career as a lawyer again after twenty years to defend his longtime friend, O.J. Simpson.) Kris didn't come with us; she had caught a bug.

We loved the quaint little Cabo marketplace that teemed with artists and craftsmen selling their wares. As we walked among the many stalls, my spirits lightened. But Nicole's unbelievable statement, "I'm afraid O.J.'s going to end up killing me," still hung in the air. No matter how hard I tried, no matter how engrossed I became in the silver jewelry that I love to buy on trips to Cabo, my mind was churning.

I knew that O.J. loved Nicole. He'd told me so many times. But whenever I pointed this out to Nicole, she answered: "Faye, he doesn't really love me. It's taken a long time for me to have the maturity to understand the truth—and the truth is that O.J. is obsessed with me. He's *beyond* obsessed. And that's not really love."

Nicole had evolved into this new, independent woman during the year she'd been separated, then divorced from O.J. Her sense of their seventeen-year history was that O.J. had married her because he needed to possess her. In his words, he "had to have her." He had married her, but he had never gained total possession of her. What he had was the submissive wife, mother, and enthusiastic sexual partner he had created. And for years, Nicole had accepted that role as her whole life. But, inevitably, when she finally started growing up, she rebelled. O.J. could never accept this.

The fury that possessed him whenever she behaved like a normal wife and partner—like complaining bitterly when he openly had sexual liaisons with other women—erupted out of his belief that she was literally his possession. O.J. was genuinely astounded at being questioned. As his rage mounted, he would turn the blame around and condemn Nicole for getting him angry, totally bypassing the issue of how he had wronged her.

The Cabo marketplace was a sun-drenched riot of crowds and color. I kept glancing at Nicole, and I knew she'd blocked out everything. She was oblivious to the chaos churning through my mind. I thought, *How does she do it? And why had she even started this reconciliation attempt?*

After all, Nicole had initiated the idea with O.J. Despite the beatings and the womanizing, something always led her back to him. I felt like crying. I also felt like shaking her, and asking, "Why did you wait so long to tell me what you told me last night? Why did you let it get to this point? Don't you realize how furious O.J. is going to be when he finds out that you've decided to break off your connection forever? How can you be so calm about it now?"

Suddenly, thankfully, I was distracted. Simone came running up and said, "Faye! I found the thumb rings you've been looking for. They're over here!"

She led me to one of the stalls. I was delighted when I saw exactly what I'd wanted—silver rings that are worn on the thumb. I used to wear them back in my hippie phase. Now they were in style again. I bought six—one each for the three girls, one for Kris, one for Nic, and one for myself. We were so excited. We felt very cool wearing our thumb rings. I guess I thought they'd be sort of the symbol of our girls' club: Kris, Nic, and I. I'd bought the place out, but planned to buy three more—for the others in our group—the next time I returned.

As I write these words today, I'm crying at the awful memory of something I was told three weeks after the murders by one of the Kardashian girls. She said her father had suddenly noticed that she and her sister were wearing the thumb rings. He asked where they'd come from. They told him I'd bought them as gifts in Cabo San Lucas. Kardashian then said, "That's exactly the same kind of ring that was found next to Nicole's body when the police discovered her."

I won't dwell on how deeply that renewed my grief. Anyone who has lost someone close to them could easily understand the emotional impact that statement would generate. It made me wonder, *How did that ring come off her thumb?* It was a devastating thought, conjuring up painful images of that awful death struggle.

Later, when I had time to consider Kardashian's statement more calmly, I thought, *"What kind of man would tell his daughters that rings identical to theirs had been found at the murder scene?"* It was a grotesque thing to say—but perhaps no more than the unfounded lies that someone had told to O.J. Simpson's defense team: That Nicole must have been involved in a drug deal that went wrong and that she was murdered by the dealers. This idiotic scenario evaporated like all the other desperate red herrings Robert Shapiro flung to their trained seals in the media.

* * *

After shopping the silver market, Nicole and I went back to the our villa. Neither of us felt like talking. Like many people who have suffered constant abuse at some point in life, we knew what to do when trouble loomed. We started blocking and found some distraction. "Hey, Nic," I said. "What do you say we go dancing tonight?"

Now that was a night on the town. The first place we hit was named Squid Row, and the minute we went out on the dance floor together, a crowd of guys congregated. They all looked like little boys standing at a candy counter.

Nic and I checked them out, sort of looking without looking. Not a hunk among them. "No wonder they call this *Squid* Row," I giggled. We finally let a couple of the more attractive guys dance with us. But they wanted to nest and we wanted to dance, so we shook them and moved on to The Giggling Marlin.

It was wild that night—standing room only at the huge bar and every table in the place taken. We strolled in, Nic looking very cute in her usual uniform of tank top, ripped jeans, and boots. I wore a similar outfit, minus the rips. Guys started swarming, asking us to dance.

The Giggling Marlin could be fun. You met everyone from beach bums to wrinkled-up, nut-brown Mexican fisherman—with a sprinkling of millionaires. This was one of the better nights.

The pounding music made the dance floor tingle under our feet. Nic and I were fending off some revved-up guys when suddenly she made eye contact with a man who was walking right toward us through the crowd. He was your basic tall, dark, and handsome, and I thought, *Not bad, Nic.* Nic ate him up in an instant when he came up and said, with a boyish charm, "Can I take you ladies away from all this?"

Nic started to glow. I sort of rolled my eyes at her, but I knew what was going on. Most times, Nic liked to go out on the town, have a good time talking with the boys, and then go home alone. She drew men like a magnet, and they were there whenever she needed them. But other times, like tonight, all she wanted to do was get out of her own head. That meant Nic was going to end up "doing" this guy.

He introduced himself as Josh, then led us back to his table. There were two or three other guys in his party, one from Los Angeles, Don. After introductions all around, Nic dragged Josh out onto the dance floor. I knew she'd be gone for a while. A guy came up to the table and started coming on strong to me. He wasn't obnoxious, but just wouldn't take "no" for an answer. Finally she came back and rescued me. The great thing about Nic is she has three ways of talking: She's either giggly and happy, totally silent, or totally blunt. She told this guy: "Leave her alone. She's not interested. "The guy backed off a little but not much.

Nic was sitting on Josh's lap. They were kissing and cuddling, so I got up and sat on Don's lap, which he seemed to liked very much. He'd been trying to get me to be with him, too. He made a move to kiss me, but I put him off. He was far less persistent than the other guy, who finally did get the message. Nicole flashed me a grin. She thought my problem was kind of funny.

We finally left. I diplomatically dumped Don. Nicole had the magnificent Josh firmly in tow. We went to our villa, and I headed for my bedroom. Nic whispered, "See you in the morning."

"I can't wait for the details!" I answered. And off I went to sleep alone in that soothing Cabo San Lucas night air.

* * *

The next morning I snuggled in Nic's bed as she gushed about her night with Josh. I knew right away it was no big deal. She liked him; she'd enjoyed him sexually; but she wasn't passionate about him, although he took away the pain.

Then she told me, "O.J.'s been sending me faxes from Puerto Rico."

"Oh, God, really?"

"Yeah. He wants me to call him."

"What are you going to do?"

"Fucking ignore him. I told you. It's over. Totally over."

God, I thought, *O.J.'s going to go crazy when she doesn't return his faxes or call him.* And I was certain that she wouldn't. When Nicole withdraws, she withdraws. No phone calls. No contact. Absolutely nothing.

A shiver went through me. This was going to be bad trouble. Here O.J. thought he had Nicole back in the palm of his hand, that love had truly bloomed in Cabo San Lucas before he'd left for Puerto Rico to film *The Frogmen*.

I left our villa alone and went over to see Kris and the kids for a while. She was still ill. Later, Nicole and I had lunch down by the beach. Josh joined us. His fascination with Nic was almost painful to watch. I picked up the disappointment in his face when Nicole said, "I think I'm probably going to leave tomorrow or the next day. Are you ready for Los Angeles again, Faye?"

"Sure. Let's talk tomorrow."

That night, Nicole and Josh asked me to dinner.

I declined. Josh was headed for his last-ever magical night with Nicole, and I figured, *Why not let him enjoy it alone?*

I had a gnawing worry about how things were going to be back home. Once Nic got back to town, O.J. could telephone her. And I knew it was going to get really nasty then. Dammit, I thought, *Why are we always worrying about what O.J. is going to do next?*

Chapter 16

TERROR

*B*ack home, I swung back into the Beverly Hills "young matron" routine: charity work, participation in Francesca's after-school activities, and helping Christian run his medical practice. Things were quiet for a week or so. Nicole and I had a few shopping trips, lunches, and dinners, but we didn't do anything special. I was very involved in Francesca's activities. She was president of her fourth-grade Ecology Club and mothers Valerie Harper, Joanne Koplin, Jeanne Cohen, and I were staging an ecology play at the school.

When Nicole and I got back to Los Angeles, we heard reports that O.J. had been doing what we called his "radar tracking," scoping out the girls in

Puerto Rico. One friend of ours, an ex-Navy seal who was filming *The Frogmen* with O.J. told us, "During those whole two weeks he was trying to "do" every babe around."

On the sixth day, O.J. phoned me from Puerto Rico.

"I've been calling her every day, Faye...What's going on?" His voice was tense, angry. "I can't believe this!"

I calmed him down and called Nicole. She casually admitted O.J. had been calling incessantly, and she'd said things like, "Leave me alone. Obviously I just don't want to talk right now."

The next day O.J. phoned me again. He started in right away, his usual rap. "What have I done to deserve this, Faye? What's wrong with Nicole? You've got to tell me what's going on."

I couldn't tell him what was going on. He would have gone nuts. Nicole made me promise that I wouldn't say anything to warn him she was splitting up for good. I just said, "O.J., look...I don't know what's going on with Nicole. I just know she seems withdrawn. She's not even talking to me about what's going on inside her." He didn't believe me.

As O.J. phoned me day in and day out, I tried to keep him cool. One day I made the mistake of saying frankly that I really couldn't help him. He became very upset with me.

"Don't lie to me," he growled. "You always know what's happening with Nicole." He got very abusive, then boasted like a megalomaniac. He said, "There's fifty million women out there...and every one of them wants to be with me." Then he added, "But I'm monogamous to Nicole."

One day he implored, "Faye, if she's going to leave me, tell me now. I can't take it. I won't go back there, I'll go to Florida. I can't take it if she's going to leave me. If she is, I won't come back to L.A. I just don't want to come back and have the bomb dropped on me. It'll make me crazy."

I told him not to worry, that everything was fine. Today I feel guilty about that. Should I have told him that she was leaving him? Would he have then flown to Florida, where Paula Barbieri lived, and given up on Nicole? My best guess is that it wouldn't have changed a thing. The more I look back on it, the more I believe it was pre-ordained.

* * *

Nicole and I were watching *Entertainment Tonight* at my house. They were showing the filming of *The Frogmen*. I asked Nicole, "Does it feel strange to watch him—now that you're ready to let him go?"

Nicole said, "I feel sad and slightly scared. I look at his arms and think, 'God, are these going to be the arms that will kill me someday?' "

Incredibly, O.J. phoned me while we were still watching *E.T.* He must have tried Nicole's place first and found out she wasn't at home. He didn't know she was sitting right next to me.

I told him I was watching him on TV. "Do you think Nicole's seeing it?"

"I don't know, O.J."

"Well, do you think it would make her want to call me?"

"I would think she'd call. And I'm pretty sure she's watching."

"Well, we'll see," he said. "I'll call you later, if she calls me or not."

But Nicole didn't call O.J., and he was really hurt. He called me back later, after Nicole had left, and sounded depressed. "This is so typical of Nicole. She doesn't even care. She doesn't want to critique the show or tell me how well I did."

During one phone call, O.J. asked if I was planning a birthday party for Christian. I didn't want O.J. to come in his present mood, but there was no way I could duck it. He and Christian usually got along very well.

I said, "O.J., you're not due back in Los Angeles until, Saturday, April 30. And Christian's birthday is April 28. That's the day I've hired the caterers and sent out invitations for." O.J. said, "Cancel everything, I want to be there. I want to be part of Christian's birthday."

What was I going to do? All I needed was to tell O.J. I wouldn't change Christian's party to accommodate him—and then have him roll into town and find out Nicole had left him.

I called Nicole immediately. "Nic, I can't believe what I just did. I postponed Christian's birthday party because O.J. isn't coming until April 30, and he insists on being there."

She blew up. "There he goes, Faye, manipulating every situation. And you let him do it. He has the nerve to tell you to postpone a birthday party at your house and you go along with it!"

I tried to explain. "Nic, this is Christian's birthday. I want it to be nice. We don't know O.J.'s frame of mind. Every time he calls me, he sounds obsessed and crazy. Please, don't break up with him until after the party.

"I knew if I'd told O.J. that I wouldn't postpone the party, he would have flipped out and come flying back to L.A. What you need to do right now is make sure you're protected from him. You have *got* to talk to your attorney and your therapist."

Nicole promised me she'd make the calls, but I now believe she never did.

On April 30, she went to the airport to pick up O.J. When they arrived at my house to join our party of about forty people, I just couldn't believe Nicole. She played the dutiful wife perfectly! Everyone was surprised at how loving they were. They never fought once. Nicole sat on the floor next to O.J.'s chair, looking up at him adoringly.

Even O.J.'s behavior was different that night. He's usually the most sociable man in the world. But he hardly talked to anyone. All his attention focused on Nicole. At one point, they disappeared into my bedroom for a half hour. It was incredible behavior!

The next day Nicole called to tell me what a great time they'd had. I finally asked her, "Nic, you guys looked so together last night. I'm confused again. Is everything okay?"

'We had a really nice time last night, Faye. But I haven't changed my mind. By the way, tonight O.J. wants to go check out the House Of Blues."

I was astounded! "Nic, I just don't get you at all! Usually, when someone's going to leave someone, they act like they're not too happy. Or am I losing my mind? What is it about you two? How can you tell me you absolutely won't stay with O.J., then say things are great and you're going off with him to the House of Blues? What's going on?" Nic just laughed. She didn't want to talk about it.

I tried to figure out exactly what was going on with them now. Nicole kept telling me it was over, but she kept going out with him.

Poor Nic. When it came to O.J., she just couldn't make up her mind. She'd get tough, but she always had that soft spot. O.J. knew it—and when O.J. wanted to be charming, he was hard to resist. I knew he'd been sending her flowers, gifts, and even catered breakfasts.

No one could court a woman like The Juice. He had his game down perfectly. It was candy, jewelry, champagne, caviar, room service, and romance—or whatever it took. O.J.'s suave superstar style had seduced some of the world's most beautiful women, but the adoration of "fifty million women" wasn't enough. He had that weak spot for the one woman who dared to walk out on him—and was about to do it again.

Two days after a lovey-dovey night at the House of Blues, Nicole blew up at him. She'd had it with the apologies, the amends, the promises to be monogamous, and the vow to seek help for his violent tendencies.

* * *

The phone rang. It was O.J. Now what? He started right on me. "I told you, Faye, you better tell me if she's going to leave me. She's acting weird, getting in my face. I'm going crazy here. She's starting to hint that it's all over between us again. I'm really pissed at you. Faye, you promised you'd tell me if she's going to leave me. I trusted you to tell me. Why didn't you?"

What the hell had happened now? I knew I'd find out soon. Whenever they had trouble, they both used me as the mediator—so I expected Nicole to be on the phone at any second. I vamped and tried to calm O.J. down.

"O.J. you know what you need to do right now? You need to go see a shrink. I can't be your shrink. I don't have a degree in therapy. Nicole has been cool. She's been fine. Everything is going to be okay. I'm not saying you guys are going to get remarried next week. But if you just kind of chill out and calm down right now maybe you can get some clarity, and if you can go to your shrink maybe he'll help you gain some understanding. In fact, I think you and Nicole should go and see a shrink together."

O.J. started agreeing with me and said he'd call right away for an emergency session. I hadn't even known he'd had a therapist. I hung up, surprised that Nicole hadn't phoned me yet. Maybe she didn't think it was any big deal. She'd probably just given O.J. a hard time, and he went off the deep end because he sensed she was moody. Later that day, O.J. called again. This time he sounded upbeat.

"Faye, I just got back from the shrink. Guess what? He thinks I've just been overwhelming Nicole. She'll eventually come back to me, but I need to give her a little bit of space."

O.J. sounded fine; he was calm. We talked for a while, and he ended up telling me, "I'm going to be patient no matter what it takes, Faye, no matter what I have to do. I want to be back with my wife. And if I have to eat crow for a while, I will."

Great. O.J.'s calm; he's cool. Now he had some hope. Wonderful. Maybe I'll get some peace.

I'm such a dreamer. Nicole rang me about an hour later. "Oh, hi, Nic," I chirped, "I was just going to call you. Let's go shopping and..."

Nicole cut in. "I told him."

Isn't it strange how you know exactly what

someone means, but you ask the question anyway.

"What do you mean you told him?"

"O.J. started in on his obsessive behavior again, Faye. I kept trying to tell him that maybe it's not cool right now to get together, and maybe we should go back to giving each other some space. But he just won't listen. He just starts saying all that PMS crap. He keeps saying, 'Oh, you're just having your period.' "

I sighed. How many times had I heard that one? Whenever Nicole got in his face, O.J. blamed it on PMS. He literally clocked her periods. It was his excuse for Nicole going against him. He just couldn't acknowledge that *anything* was his fault. So *everything* became her fault, courtesy of PMS. O.J. would say to me, "Faye, when Nicole's PMS'ing, she wants nothing to do with me. Everything is 'Fuck you' and 'Leave me alone.' "

This was getting weird. I told Nicole, "Don't push him now. I mean it. He's getting scary. Stop telling him you'll never be with him again. If you tell him that, I think you're getting into deep water. Your fears that he could kill you might come true."

"Faye, I tried that. I told him this wasn't about PMS. I said to him, 'Right now, you're just too much of a man for me, O.J. You are so obsessed it frightens me. I no longer trust you when you say you will be only with me. All of our fights were about your affairs, and the only reason I came back to you is that you said you were going to be monogamous. I don't believe that any more. I hear stories about you and Paula.' Faye, I tried the slow disconnect, but it didn't work. So I just told him how it's going to be."

"Oh God, Nic. What have you done?"

How many times have I heard the cliché "my blood ran cold"? But that's what it felt like when Nicole told me: "I finally faced up to him. I told him, 'O.J., I never ever want to see you again. Get out of my life. Get away from me. Get the fuck away from me. And don't ever call me again. You are one sick individual.' "

I wanted to scream. I wanted to run away. I was terrified. I couldn't handle the emotion flooding through me. "Nic, Goddamn it, why? Why did you do that?"

"I'll tell you why," she snapped. " 'He called me up awhile ago and said, 'Nicole, I just finished talking to my shrink.' So I said to him, 'O.J., did you talk to him honestly? Did you tell him everything that has happened to us? Did you talk to him about how you abused me, how you beat me?'

"You know what he said, Faye? He said, 'Well,

what does that have to do with anything? We're in a new era here. This is all about going forward.' "

Her voice had taken on an undertone of near-hysteria. "Are you getting the picture here Faye? O.J. never talked to the shrink about abuse at all. But I'm not surprised. That stuff's too close to the bone for him. He never admits to that kind of thing. It would make him look bad—and God forbid O.J. should ever look bad to strangers. That's when I decided this whole thing is hopeless. O.J. is never going to change. He wants to get me back, then screw everything in skirts—Tawny and Paula and God knows who else. And you know the rumors about him doing it with hookers. What about AIDS? If I'm with him, and I complain about his women, he's going to beat me. And maybe someday he'll beat me to death."

She sounded almost resigned. "So that's my choice, Faye. I think he'll kill me if I stay with him, so if he's going to kill me because I'm leaving, I might as well face it now."

Oh Jesus! I took a deep breath. "Nic, tell me the truth. Did you do what you agreed to do before? Did you tell your attorney about this stuff so he could tip off the police? Did you talk to your shrink? And O.J.'s shrink? Tell me the truth, Nicole. I'm freaking out, too. I just can't take this. I'm so scared he's going to hurt you."

My other phone line rang. I put Nicole on hold. It was O.J., yelling, cursing.

"Faye, that fucking bitch, she told me she never wants to be with me again..."

"O.J., listen "

He cut me off. "If she's really serious about this, and I find out she's with any other man before August, *I'll kill her*!"

"Whoa! O.J., what are you saying?"

"I can't take this, Faye, I can't take this. I mean it. *I'll kill that bitch*."

"O.J., hold on..."

I punched the other line. "Nicole, O.J.'s on the other line; I'll call you back."

I got back on the line with O.J. He was really out of control now, and there wasn't much I could do except try to calm him down. "Faye, I know what's going on here. She wants nothing to do with me. So she's got to be with another man."

'O.J., she's not with anybody else. First of all, she has no interest in being with anybody else. Right now, Nicole is introspective; you need to give her space, some time to put things together for herself."

"I know—but what about me? What about me, Faye? Why do I have to be in a relationship like this?"

I said, "You don't have to be in this relationship.

You chose to be in it. And you chose to stay in it. Just leave her alone. Give Nicole some time. She'll come up with her own conclusions about what's going on. And you'll be the first to know, O.J."

Every conversation with O.J. Simpson was déjà vu. Everything we said had been said a thousand times before. Sure enough, O.J. came right back at me with his same old rap, turning the situation around and focusing it on the most important person in the world—O.J. Simpson.

"What are you talking about, Faye? That's bullshit! I didn't ask to be in this relationship. I divorced Nicole. Then she came back to me when I was perfectly happy with Paula. She begged me to get together again. She instigated this whole thing. She forced me into this, Faye. I was happy with Paula. I mean, really happy.

"Who does Nicole think she is, anyway? I was being monogamous. There are fifty million women out there who want O.J. Simpson, but I was playing straight!"

It was just too much. "O.J., don't lie to me," I yelled. "You know damn well that I know damn well what you've been doing. Don't you think we hear things? Don't you think those fifty million women talk and gossip? Don't you think the stories about sleeping with O.J. Simpson filter back to Nicole?

"How the hell do you think that makes her feel, O.J.? Stop and think about that. All I'm hearing here is you, you, you. Can I just remind you of something? You've told me you'd kill Nicole. I can't believe any man could say that about the mother of his children, about the woman he supposedly loves. Did you mean it when you said you'd kill her? I mean, really mean it?"

"You heard me," he roared. "If she's with another man, *I'll kill her.* You tell her she'd better play her role and look like my wife until August. Stay away from any man until August. You tell her that, Faye!"

What was all this August stuff? I'd ask Nic later.

"O.J., after what you just said to me, and to Nicole, how can you expect her to want to be with you? She's afraid of you, O.J. You've beaten her so many times."

O.J. brushed it off. "That was in the past. I haven't touched her lately."

The phone call ended a few minutes later. I called Nicole and said, "Look, I really don't know what to do here. I feel like my hands are tied. O.J.'s acting crazy, and I'm really nervous about you. I'm coming over."

It was a smart idea getting out of there. Before I could go out that awful day, I had at least four more calls from O.J., and I know he called me several times while I was away from home.

I phoned my doctor and asked for a prescription of Valium. A voice inside kept telling me not to do it. When you're suffering from the disease of drug addiction, taking Valium or any drug is a rotten idea. But, dear God, the pressure I felt was beyond belief; I had no option.

I felt like my brain was going to burst through my skull. I couldn't stop shaking and crying. Valium was the only way I could calm myself down. I had to get myself under control and figure out a way to help Nicole.

I just could not believe this nightmare was happening, that I was trapped in this hellish, never-ending drama of threatened violence. The only way out was to leave my best friend. But there was no way I would have considered doing that.

I grabbed a purse, jumped into my Jeep, and stopped off at the pharmacy. My nerves felt as if they were crawling right out through my skin. I asked the pharmacist for a glass of water and took my Valium right there.

A few minutes later I got to Nicole's house. She opened the door, and emotion engulfed us. We hugged and cried, reassuring each other that we would somehow escape this unending terror bearing down on us. We momentarily suffered what amounted to a joint breakdown, and it took us a while to calm down, to speak rationally.

"Okay, Nicole. It is what it is. We've got to save your life. How can we do it?"

Nicole didn't want to hear it. She just kept saying, "Fuck him. He's a bastard, and I'm not going to let him scare me."

That was Nicole. When she got her back up, she turned stubborn, fearless. But irrational defiance was the last thing she needed now. I pleaded with her. "Nicole, let's just calm down and get this thing organized. Let's go to Laguna. And on the way down, let's figure out exactly what we're going to do about this. We can have somebody look after our kids, or we can take the kids. Please Nicole, we've got the money. Let's just go. There's nothing keeping us here."

Remembering O.J.'s emphasis on August, I asked her about it. What was the significance of August?

"O.J takes off for New York in August,"' she told me. "He's usually there four or five months doing his broadcasting. So he wants me to stay away from men until he goes to New York. Then he'll start screwing every woman in sight."

When I pressed Nicole about getting out of town and staying in Laguna, she refused. We went out to Rosti's to get something to eat. No matter how hard I tried to persuade her, Nicole refused to take O.J.'s threat seriously enough to leave town.

"Nic, I don't know how to help you here, except to tell you again. You need to talk to your shrink. You need to talk to his shrink. You need to call an attorney, and you need to call the police. Tell people what's going on. If he knows you're going public with this, he won't kill you. No man in his right mind is going to do that."

So that was the plan we decided on. Nicole swore to me she'd inform her attorney, both psychiatrists, and the authorities. But she still had doubts about the plan. Nicole was actually afraid that O.J. would get even angrier if he found out she was going public, even in a limited way. O.J.'s image was still the most important thing in his life. He lived for what others thought of him.

I made Nicole promise me faithfully that she wouldn't be with any men until O.J. left for New York in August. It was the best I could do; I certainly couldn't put her in a straitjacket. But I still had one overwhelming worry.

"You know what makes me nervous, Nic? Even if you aren't actually with another man, you know how O.J. gets. He thinks any man you talk to or look at is "doing you" sexually. I just don't think he can tell the difference between reality and his imagination. I'm worried he might just get the idea in his head that you were with someone and kill you for it."

Nicole didn't agree. She believed that if she kept her part of the bargain, if she wasn't with, or caught sexually with, another man until August, O.J. would leave her alone.

"Okay, Nic. But you swear, right? You swear you won't be with any man sexually until O.J. leaves for New York?"

Nic laughed. "I swear, Faye. Of course I swear."

Chapter 17

THE BUSH SYNDROME

I had no way of knowing it at the time, but after
Nicole's death I learned that May 4, was the day
O.J. went into a Los Angeles knife shop and purchased the now infamous fifteen-inch German
stiletto that ended up in a mysteriously sealed en-
velope given to the court.

Is it significant that O.J. bought this knife just
weeks before the murders? Perhaps. To me, it matters little who or what killed Nicole. What matters
is that I can't bring her back.

* * *

Now O.J. put the pressure on, hard. He started
stalking Nicole. Up until now, there had only been

what we called the "Bush Syndrome." Whenever Nicole and I were in her house, we'd always check to see if O.J. was hiding in the bushes. We'd look out the window when we were in the living room and say, "Is O.J. out there?" Nicole had caught O.J. in the bushes spying on her more than once.

Around this time, two incidents occurred that intensified my fears for Nicole. We'd chatted earlier, and she'd told me she had to pick up some shoes for Sydney, then go to Aaron Brothers, a frame shop on Lincoln Boulevard. Nicole had purchased two Picasso prints, one for her and one for me, then heard there was a two-for-one sale at the frame shop. Typical Nicole, she was going to zip right across town and save some money.

As she drove, she looked in her rearview mirror and saw the notorious white Bronco that would soon become familiar to every television viewer in America. Nicole sighed. It was O.J. She ignored him thinking, *He'll just figure I'm out shopping and give up.*

O.J. stayed behind her all the way to the frame shop. Then—as she put it to me later, "Just to fuck with him"—she waited until the last second to turn. As she cut the wheel hard left and darted into the parking lot, O.J. almost lost it. Totally confused, he had to brake hard to avoid hitting another car. Nicole turned and shot him a look of pure loathing. For an instant, O.J.'s eyes met hers. Then he drove off.

Nicole called me from her car phone. "O.J.'s been following me."

I said, "Oh, great. What have you been doing? Is there anything you've done I should know about?"

"God, Faye. I haven't done anything. There was a two-for-one sale at Aaron Brothers."

Nicole and I started laughing like crazy fools as she described the expression on his face as he almost hit the car. "Maybe he'll just stick to the bushes now!" giggled Nic.

My other line rang. I knew it was O.J. It was the old pattern—in times of crisis Nicole and O.J. would both call me, sometimes simultaneously. Then I'd have to pretend to O.J. that I wasn't on the phone with Nicole—but I always let Nicole know I was on with O.J. Now I put O.J. on hold and switched back to Nicole. "Nic, Nic, O.J. is obsessing on the other line. I'll call you back."

I clicked Nicole off, then hit the other line.

"O.J., what's wrong?"

He was steaming. "Faye, I almost got in a car accident. And it's all Nicole's fault. I was driving along and just by coincidence I saw Nicole driving down Lincoln Boulevard. So I was going to say hello, and she turned real sharp, and I almost hit another car."

"So what's the problem, O.J. Were you hurt? You didn't hit the car, did you?"

"No, but now I'm sure she thinks I was following her. I really wasn't. It was just a coincidence."

"O.J., it sounds to me like you were following her. And that is unacceptable. You don't follow people. What do you want me to say to Nicole when I talk to her? Do you want me to say, 'Oh, he was just in the area.' C'mon, O.J. we know that's not your M.O. We know how you hide in the bushes. We know you watch what we do. She's going to know you were following her."

"No, she won't! And I wasn't following her!"

I said, "Fine, fine, O.J. If you say you weren't following her, you weren't following her."

I hung up, thinking how O.J. tried to control Nicole through other people: her friends, even her family.

When he'd screw up, he'd phone one of her girlfriends, or one of her sisters. He'd plant his "excuse" with them, hoping they'd tell Nicole later. It was so manipulative, but often very effective. O.J. knew it didn't work with me because I usually spoke my mind. But as Nicole always put it, I was "more into her head than anyone else." O.J. knew I was the best pipeline into her heart, her mind, and her soul.

Now I was nervous. O.J. was actually stalking Nicole, and she'd caught him at it. It wasn't the first time. One day we'd stopped at Starbucks for cappuccino. Nicole and I loved to sit on the low wall in front of the coffee shop. It was a great place to watch life in the tiny but exquisite village of Brentwood.

Anyway, we were sipping our cappuccino with a bunch of the Starbucks boys, those gorgeous young aspiring actors and good-looking guys who worked out and had hard bodies. Nicole had a crush on one of them, who she thought was really cute. I agreed. His name was Ron Goldman, and the first time I saw him I told Nicole, "There's only one boy here who's worthy—it's Ron, and he's absolutely gorgeous!"

Nicole was pleased to hear my judgment. But looking back on it, I feel a lot of guilt. I don't know why, and I know it's irrational. Nothing I did caused Ron's murder. But it's just something that will bother me forever.

Let me answer the burning question, once and for all: Nicole and Ron Goldman were not lovers. No matter what you've read in the press, no matter what speculation has intrigued you, it's just not true. What is true is that, inevitably, Nicole was going to "do" Ron. It was something that was going to happen. But Nicole was in no rush.

* * *

In mid-May, Nicole came down with double pneumonia. The doctor ordered total bed rest. I brought flowers on her second day in bed. Dita, Nic's mother, was there. It was so amazing to see Nicole looking ill, flat on her back. She was so athletic, so vital, so full of life. This was the one girl I knew who was always physically fit.

About the fourth day, O.J. showed up at her condo. He was really laying on the charm. As Nicole's days of sickness stretched into weeks, he constantly dropped by with flowers and presents. He kept saying he needed to see the kids and how much he missed everybody.

I watched him and realized, *This is a godsend for him. She can't escape him, and he gets another chance to win her back.* I wondered if Nic's resolve to leave him forever would weaken. Frankly, I thought it might. O.J. had a chance. It's hard for a woman to resist flowers, presents, and cheerful visits when she's too sick to move.

But Nicole remained resolved. She told me, "I know he's trying to be nice, but nothing is going to change my mind. He's the same O.J."

May 19 was Nicole's birthday, but she was too sick to celebrate. Kris and I told her we'd have a birthday lunch as soon as she got well. I spent that weekend at Nicole's house because Christian and I were fighting. For me, romance had become something you read about in novels.

Nic kept saying that the reason she'd come down with double pneumonia was the stress from this strength-sapping cat-and-mouse game with O.J. I don't want to blame O.J. for my problems with Christian, but the nervousness I felt was affecting my daily life, too.

Slowly, cocaine was exerting its insidious grip on me. Christian, who hated drugs of any kind, was growing progressively tense and impatient. What was I supposed to tell him? "Wait until August, honey. I'll give it up. Things will be fine when O.J. goes to New York, sweetheart." I hadn't been easy to live with lately and I knew it.

Finally, Nicole got better. On May 27, a Friday night, we went out and hit a few of the usual spots: Bar One, the Roxbury. It was a quiet weekend. We did a little dancing, went out for cappuccino Saturday afternoon, and dinner Sunday night. O.J. kept his distance. And I thought, *August is only two months away. Perhaps it'll be a quiet summer.*

How wrong I was.

* * *

On a sunny Beverly Hills morning, I dropped Francesca off at her school, stopped by Starbucks for my morning cappuccino, then headed down Bundy Drive toward Christian's office. Nicole lived on Bundy, and as I passed her house I glanced over automatically—and my heart almost stopped. Instinctively my foot stabbed for the brake. I went by slowly. My heart started up again, pounding furiously. There, outside Nicole's house, was Marcus Allen's car.

For a split second I thought of stopping. Then I thought, *What am I going to do? Drop in for a cup of coffee?* I drove on. How could she do this? I felt panicky, fearful. At first I went into denial. Was I mistaken? Perhaps it wasn't Marcus's car. This was ridiculous. I knew damn well it was.

Beneath my shock was the feeling that I'd just witnessed something that would end in tragedy. But was this a tragedy or a bad soap opera? How could Nicole take this terrible chance after O.J. had threatened to kill her if she dated another man?

Why did she reach out for the one who was totally taboo? And with O.J. just blocks away.

Emotions whipped through me so crazily that I almost ran onto a curb. I considered stopping to collect my thoughts. I slowed, concentrated on my driving, and finally reached Christian's office.

I launched into work with a fury, I didn't want a moment to think. I knew if I started looking at the clock I'd scream. Usually I called Nicole every day around noon. I wanted to call right now, but I had no desire to talk while Marcus was still in the house. He'd probably be gone by noon.

Every time I paused in my work, my fears came rushing back. This had been a shock, but not totally unexpected. Weeks before, CiCi had told me Marcus was back in town, and she thought Nicole was seeing him. I sort of blew it off at the time, not taking it seriously. Looking back, I know now it was just something I didn't want to hear. It was unthinkable. But the unthinkable had happened.

Goddamn it, Nicole, I thought. *What's in your head? Will I ever know what's in your head?*

Finally it was noon. I took a deep breath. It was time to call the woman who usually shared every intimate secret with me. But she hadn't shared this time. I dreaded having this conversation. I called. Nicole answered.

"Hello?"

"Hi, Nicole."

"Faye, hi!" She sounded great. "So, how ya doin'?"

"Great."

Well, so much for the pleasantries, I thought. *I wish we could go on like this, and talk about shopping and the kids—but we can't, so here goes.*

"Nicole—was that Marcus's car outside your house?"

A pause. Then, in an apprehensive voice, "Yeah, Faye, yeah..."

I took a deep breath. She'd admitted it. *Okay,* I told myself. *Don't lose it, Faye. Don't push her too hard. Try to keep this as sane as possible.* A rising tide of emotion choked me. I took another deep breath.

"Nicole, what are you doing? You're playing with fire! Didn't we make a deal? This is something you just don't do. Don't you know how dangerous this is?"

"Faye, I dig him. He makes me feel really good. And I'm entitled to happiness."

'Yes, you're entitled to happiness. That's what I want for you. But you may be signing your death warrant. How do you think this can lead to anything but O.J. blowing up and maybe carrying out his threat? Nicole, even if he doesn't kill you, what do you think he is going to do? This is even worse than before, if that's possible. Marcus just got married to Kathryn, what, six months ago? You remember, don't you? It was a quiet little ceremony with about a million people up at O.J.'s house! Look, I'm not your mother, but you're doing something really off the wall here."

"Faye, I didn't ask for your advice. If I want your advice, I'll ask you."

Now she'd pissed me off. "Don't give me that, Nicole. You've asked for my advice through this whole thing. We plotted, we planned, you wanted my help every step of the way, and I gave it to you. You *swore* you'd be cool until August, Nicole. Do you remember?! Now you're seeing Marcus Allen and saying, 'Faye, I don't need your advice.' Where do you get off suggesting that I don't have a right to think this is bad news?"

I knew it was pointless to argue anymore right now. When in doubt, go back to the banal.

"Look, Nic, I think we really have to talk about this some more. What do you say we have lunch at Rosti's?"

"Oh, great. Then we can go over and buy the flowers at Rolling Green Nursery for Sydney's Communion."

"Okay, great..."

We made the date and I hung up, thinking, *Do guys do this too? Have a crisis then decide to go shopping? I sighed. Why not? What else could I do* if Nic refused to stop seeing Marcus?

At lunch, we talked it through some more. It ended up as it always did these days, me pleading with Nicole to use her head.

"Look, Nic. Don't you realize that it's going to be really bad if O.J. gets wind of this?"'

"O.J.'s been laying low lately, Faye. The children and I haven't even seen him. I think he might be out of town."

"Yeah, maybe. But we don't know that, do we? What we *do* know about O.J. is that he hides in the bushes. He follows you in his car. He might be having you followed now by someone else. And if he saw Marcus's car outside your house in plain sight, he'll be having Marcus followed. Just promise me—swear to me again—that you won't see Marcus anymore after today. Please, Nic."

"Faye, I deserve some happiness."

Chapter 18

THE BOND

Brentwood, California
May 1994

*H*ow can I describe the intensity of my relationship with Nicole, particularly toward the end?
We had become more than friends. Call it what
you will, bonded sisters, soulmates, confidantes—
some palpable force, some emotion I'd never experienced, drew us together.

I knew it was love, of course. Nicole was my best
friend, and I loved her dearly. In those last days I
found myself thinking of this constantly. When I
became aware of that, I dismissed it as a manifesta-
tion of my growing nervousness and fears for her
safety. Nicole, the most loving creature I've ever
encountered, often talked of "falling in love" with
me or told me how much she loved me. "I've

never felt more spiritually connected to anyone, Faye."

I laughed. 'Oh, Nic! Falling in love? What a thing to say? I'm a girl!"

I have never had thoughts of physical love with another woman. When Nic talked of "falling in love," I remember thinking, *Could I ever do that? Even with Nicole?*

It was more than the fear of crossing a sexual line; my relationship with Nicole was precious. I would never let anything alter or ruin it. Yet the thought lingered in the air: *Could it actually enhance our bond?*

I could almost hear the voice of my mother, the religious fanatic, warning, God would not allow those with such thoughts into the Kingdom of Heaven. My mother's God didn't frighten me. The God I know lets me do what I feel is right in my heart. But this I know: I would never have initiated a physical relationship with a woman, even Nicole. Never in a million years.

As I write these words, I am thinking of my daughter Francesca and her reaction to them. I have always told the truth to my daughter, and I am telling the truth now, to her and to the world.

* * *

One night Nicole and I went out dancing to blow off some tension, to forget all of the weirdness and fear that had been building in the air like some far-off, inevitable storm. The music felt like it was coming from inside me. It was wonderful. Nic was laughing, abandoned, totally happy.

When we sat at our table and had a couple of tequilas, I telephoned my housekeeper. Francesca was with her father, Christian was off on a weekend motorcycle trip, and Nicole's kids were staying over with her mother. My housekeeper told me no one had called. I told her I'd be home soon and that Nicole was staying over. I asked her to draw a bath and light my candles.

"All of them?" she asked.

"Yes, all of them."

Nicole and I danced some more, had a nightcap with some friends, then drove to my place. I was in a mellow mood that night. As I walked through the door, I hit the stereo switch; Madonna's "Erotica" filled the house and pinpoints of candlelight glowed in every room.

God, I loved my house. I had decorated it to reflect the wildly romantic, exotic persona that I rarely revealed. It's done in gold leaf and black, very Egyptian, with sculptures, down-filled sofas with tassels and fringes, light carpeting, zebra skins, black and gold Roman and Egyptian chairs, a massive oriental screen, and a magnificent oriental desk. The black and gold motif carries into the bedroom. My custom-made bed is Roman, also black and gold, covered with overstuffed down pillows and a wonderful bedroll. The whole place is an expression of romance.

Nicole had never seen my place totally ablaze with candlelight. When we walked in, she said, "Wow, it's so sensual!"

I laughed. My ex-husband, Paul, had said almost the same thing years ago when we were living in San Francisco. He'd spent $100,000 decorating a huge bath, complete with Jacuzzi. Sometimes, I'd go there in the middle of the night when Paul was asleep and spend hours alone.

One night, Paul woke up at about three o'clock in the morning. Not finding me in bed, he came to the bathroom and opened the door. He gasped when he saw the room bathed in the light of fifteen large candles. The Jacuzzi had rose petals scattered over the water. And I was sitting in it, reading Sigmund Freud. As New Age music filled the room, Paul stood in the doorway a moment drinking it all in. Then he stepped inside, closed the door and said, "My God, this is the most sensual scene I've ever seen in my life."

Nicole jolted me out of my reverie with, "How about a drink?"

I poured us two tequilas, then we went into the bedroom. Nic breezed into my closet as she had a hundred times before and chose a nightie. After I'd changed, I sat on the bed and checked my answering machine. Nic sat next to me, and after a while, we were laughing and lounging, sharing confidences, and talking about nothing in particular.

At one point we were facing each other. Nic suddenly leaned over and started kissing me. My first reaction? It just felt so foreign. A woman was kissing me! It was Nicole, but it felt strange. I thought, *I don't feel disgusted or upset, but can I really let myself enjoy this? Am I going to be uptight? Am I going to break away now?* And then I thought, *No, I'm not going to do that. I'm going to let my feelings lead me...see how it goes....*

Nicole pulled back and looked into my eyes. I said, "I don't know how to do this. I don't know how..."

I was in a state of shock. But the shock wasn't strong enough to make me stop, despite underlying apprehension. I was enjoying this. Then...I wasn't scared anymore. This was Nicole. It was wonderful...being with her. It was more a spiritual bonding than anything else. I just felt like all the barriers were down between us. It was okay.

We fell asleep, and it's hard to believe what happened next.

I woke up suddenly. Something was wrong. I heard a voice outside my bedroom window. Then a flashlight lit up the windowpane!

"Jesus," I said, "what is this?"

Nicole was awake now. "Oh, my God, it's O.J.! He's spying on us!"

"Goddamn it," I screamed out to the intruder. "O.J. you can't do this!"

Then we heard somebody shouting. "Excuse me! Excuse me!...It's the police."

The police?

Next I heard something like, "This is the police...your neighbors are complaining about the loud music going on here."

I yelled out, "Sorry, officer! We'll turn the music down!"

I jumped out of bed and hit the volume control. Nic and I held our breath. We heard the sound of the police car pulling away. In the sudden silence, we cracked up and started laughing so hysterically we fell on the floor. Our only night of girlish passion, and it turns into a police raid. I thought we'd never stop laughing.

Finally we fell asleep.

Let me answer the unspoken question: No, it never happened again. The only discussion Nicole and I ever had was to acknowledge how inevitable it had seemed. And I discovered I wasn't the nervous one. Nicole worried constantly that I might be angry. In the next few days she asked me over and over if I was okay. I told her, "Nicole, nothing can take away my friendship. What am I? An innocent bystander? If I hadn't wanted to let it happen, I would have stopped it. You know I would."

"Yeah, I know. But I'm very nervous."

There's something about me that makes people feel that if I get really angry or hurt, I'll walk away forever. It's true that when things get bad, I'll often jump on a plane and disappear. But I told Nicole, "You never have to worry about that. You're in my blood!"

* * *

I'm aware there are women who don't enjoy sex, but I'm not among them. And neither was Nicole. In my case, it's fortunate, because my childhood was practically one long lecture on the evils of drink, drugs, and most of all—sex. I sometimes wonder how many women's marriages were ruined by parents who brainwashed them to believe that sex is dirty and evil.

My basic belief is that sex should be a special bond between caring people and that whatever two romantically involved adults find enjoyable and pleasurable is one bonus of nature.

I've had three husbands, two fiancés, and many lovers. But I've never had a one-night stand. I don't really approve of sport-fucking. My route to coping with pain was a combination of Valium and cocaine. (Please note that I said "was." Everybody has to grow up sometime.)

Nicole had a different approach. She was innately shy. She sometimes relied on her body to help her communicate. She enjoyed, actually needed, sex. Most women do. But it was also Nic's way to escape from pain. Men were her drug of choice.

Nicole and I both embarked on our sex lives at an early age, but for entirely different reasons. My first time was when I was sixteen and thoroughly convinced by my mother's religion that the world was going to come to an end. I didn't want to miss what I had been reading about in romance novels.

Nicole's motivation was different. Her older sister, Denise, was a great beauty and well-known model. Men adored her. Nicole felt that Denise would always outshine her, and that no man would find her attractive once he had seen her gorgeous sister.

As if that weren't enough, another sister, Dominique, was also a great beauty and made no secret of her conquests. So Nicole tried to compete in the only way she could. She would prove that she was grown up and that men really wanted her. Before long, it became common knowledge that the Brown sisters were, as O.J. later put it, "the ultimate trophies."

Nicole soon realized that she, too, was a beauty, and that her sexual nature could be a source of great enjoyment in her life. It wasn't until her marriage to O.J. started falling apart that she began to rely on sex as both a weapon and an opiate.

When Nicole and I became good friends, she had just filed for her divorce from O.J. and was starting to test the waters. But O.J. still thought he owned her and that she had no right to a life of her own.

That's one of the things I really resent. Not all men are as possessive as O.J., but most are judgmental. If they have an affair or even a casual encounter, they're just being men. But if a woman does exactly the same thing, she's—you name it— a whore, a slut, basically a bad human being. Throughout the ages, men have tyrannized women with this attitude. And we've let them. But I do believe that as women evolve and learn to be their own persons and control their own destinies, they will no longer buy into this philosophy.

The night Nicole and I were together was unique. We had both been disillusioned and deeply hurt by men and had lost trust in everything but each other. We needed the warmth, closeness, and safety of each other's arms. However, let me make it clear that neither Nicole nor I were or ever could be gay. I respect those that chose to be gay. That's their way of life, and I don't question it. But it's not for me.

Chapter 19

THE FINAL DAYS

Los Angeles, California
June 1994

I think it was Sunday, the first week in June, when I got a phone call from O.J. He was calm, and I knew that the reason behind his calmness was the conversation I'd had with him recently during one of his ranting phone calls.

I had exploded suddenly and told him, "Look, O.J. I'm sick and tired of your calling me because the minute I pick up the phone, you're screaming and yelling like a madman. You call yourself my friend. But every time I talk to you lately, all I ever hear about is me, me, me.

"Even when you knew I was feeling under the weather you never stopped to ask me how I was feeling; you just started screaming about Nicole.

"That's not acceptable anymore. If you do it again, I won't speak to you. When you call me, do not start off in a loud tone of voice I'll just hang up on you."

Somehow, on this call, O.J.'s calm, quiet tones made the conversation even more chilling. So far, he had made threats. Now, he was taking action. "I'm sending a letter to the IRS, Faye. I've had it with Nicole, and it's time to retaliate. She's been fooling the IRS into thinking she lives at my place. And you know she's committed tax fraud. She's either going to pay $90,000 in taxes to the IRS, or she's going to jail."

I felt that all my strength had suddenly drained out of me. Did this man ever stop inflicting pain on everyone around him? I knew what O.J. was talking about. I'm no tax expert. Obviously, neither was Nicole, but I knew she'd gotten herself into a bad tax situation when she'd initiated the reconciliation attempt with O.J.

Nicole explained to me that when she'd sold a condominium she owned in San Francisco, which she leased to tenants, she owed the IRS $90,000 in capital gains taxes unless she immediately bought another property for business purposes. She bought the condo on Bundy Drive intending to lease it out and move back to O.J.'s place on Rockingham. So she put down the Rockingham address on her tax return, figuring that's where she'd be living. Well, that never happened. Instead she stayed in the Bundy condo, in the home she was supposed to be leasing out.

Nicole had to find another place to live, or she was going to have to immediately pay $90,000 to the IRS. O.J. knew that would really hurt her. That $90,000 was almost exactly what Nicole had in the bank. She had paid cash for the Bundy condo, so she didn't have a lot of cash left.

"O.J., I can't believe what I'm hearing. How could you stoop this low?"

O.J. snapped, "This is something I just can't be a part of anymore, Faye. She's not my wife, and she's not going to be my wife. She's made that quite clear to me. So I want her to face all the pain she's made me face."

I tried to reason with him. "I understand you're upset with Nicole, O.J. But from my point of view as a mother, let me ask you why you would want to do this to your children? Don't you think they've been uprooted enough? Why don't you just wait awhile, let her lease the place out, and stop threatening her with all this stuff? Why go to such extremes?"

Now he was ranting and screaming. "You know,

why, Faye. It's because she doesn't want to be with me anymore. And I just can't be her friend anymore. I want her to be in as much pain as possible. Without me, she's nothing. Let her live in reality for a while so she'll appreciate how good she had it with me."

I screamed back at him, "O.J., I think you'd better go back to your shrink."

I slammed the phone down. Then I drove over to Nicole's, planning to stay there awhile because Christian and I were having problems. When she heard about O.J.'s latest threat, her reaction was just like mine. "How could he do this to his own children?"

Hounding Nicole and threatening her, causing trouble for her was O.J.'s normal way of doing things. It was a fact of life, and she'd gotten used to it. But he'd never made a threat to directly undermine the welfare of his own children.

Nicole and I didn't make it into a big drama. Both of us felt he was just blowing off steam once again and wouldn't *really* call the IRS. Nonetheless, Nicole phoned her real estate agent and told her she needed someone to lease the Bundy condo fast! She explained she'd been trying to lease the place to her friend, Cora Fishman, who was in the process of separating from her husband, but that hadn't worked out.

The bombshell dropped the next day. A letter from O.J.'s lawyer arrived. It restated O.J.'s threat, this time in legalese. The message was clear: O.J. was going to call the IRS and turn Nicole in for tax fraud.

Nicole exploded! I had never seen her so upset, so furious. Even she could not believe this viciousness by O.J. This time, O.J. was attacking the children, basically saying: "I'll put you through the ordeal of throwing all three of you out of the home you love."

Shortly after the letter arrived, Nicole told me, she and O.J. were raging at each other over the phone. He snarled: "This is it. This is the last time I'm going to try to be nice. If you don't realize how wonderful I am to you, then it's time you learned what real life is like."

Nicole's response was: "Just get out of my life! Just stay away from me! Because you're not the person I knew. You're a monster! I don't even know who you are!"

Was this O.J.'s last-ditch attempt to get Nicole back?

* * *

Later that day, I began to crumble under the pressure. I couldn't take this constant feeling of doom. My chest felt constricted. I had to escape. I told Nicole, "Please, let's just get out of here. Let's go to Europe. We can take our children, get a tutor. Or, you can take your kids to your mother's. And I'll take Francesca to Paul's house. The kids will be fine either way, but let's you and I get out of the country. We have the money, Nic. Let's go to St. Tropez, or to Mexico. Let's go anywhere. Let's just go!"

"No, I can't." Nicole said. "Sydney's dance recital is coming up next week."

"Damn it, Nicole, you've always got some excuse. Your safety's more important than going to the recital. So's our sanity. Your parents can take Sydney. But we've got to get out of here. We're being followed. You know it and I know it."

I didn't tell her my greatest fear, that O.J. knew she was seeing Marcus again and had a professional watching us. Today I remember how Paula Barbieri's stolen car was found with a mysterious written schedule of Nicole's movements in those final days. No one's ever proven a link to O.J., but I think O.J. had somebody on our tail.

When Nicole refused to escape from her situation, it suddenly hit me hard. I knew I absolutely had to leave without her. I told her:

"I can't be here, Nicole. I'm losing my head. I'm going out of my mind. I can't let myself stay in this terrible world you're trapped in."

Nicole didn't argue. She shook her head, and I knew what she was thinking. Over the past couple of weeks I'd slipped back into tooting and smoking coke two or three times a day and mellowing the drug's hard edge with Valium. Nicole never used the word "paranoid," but I know she thought I was overreacting.

That's exactly what Christian had been telling me. When I told him that O.J. had literally threatened over and over to kill Nicole, Christian said, "You're overreacting. Guys say things like that all the time. He doesn't mean it."

Christian and I continued to have problems at home. But I didn't want to confront him. I thought, *Leaving him might lift some of my pain.* Deep in my soul I felt something bad was coming.

When I told Nicole, she hugged me and said, "Okay, if you think you don't want to stay here, fine. But I want you to take my spare house keys and the remote for my garage so you can get back in if you change your mind. Are you going home?"

"I don't think so, Nicole. I'm going to go up to Kathy Harouche's house. Christian and I just aren't getting along."

Nicole took me downstairs and rummaged around in a drawer looking for the set of spare keys. After a moment she said, "Damn, Faye! The keys are gone. And the remote's gone. O.J.'s got them! He must have taken them last week when he was here seeing the kids."

Nicole had four sets of keys. One set was for Elvie, the maid. Cora always had one set because her kids were there a lot, and one set was for Nicole. There was an extra set that Nicole had been trying to give me for a long time. This was the set that was missing.

I felt a cold chill. "Nicole," I said shivering, "I feel we're going to be killed. We have to go. Don't you see we're being set up?"

That's when Nicole said what she'd never said openly, "Faye, maybe because you're doing drugs right now, you're a little uptight. As long as I'm not with a man, I'll be okay."

I shook my head, then hugged her good-bye and left. I drove to Kathy Harouche's house. It was up on Mulholland Drive, a gated community called Beverly Park, the most exclusive section of Beverly Hills. When the guards opened the massive gates, I drove through and literally breathed a heavy sigh of relief. As the gates closed behind me, I finally felt safe.

I kept thinking, *Oh God. If Nicole could only be here with me.* At that moment I felt like I'd abandoned her. But then I thought, *Well, she says she's going to be okay. She thinks I'm worrying too much. God, I hope she's right!* But I knew I wasn't overreacting. I'd heard O.J.'s death threats, and I believed them.

Kathy's place has always been my home away from home, my sanctuary. She and I work on charities together, and she's a great mom. She'd never take an extra drink or any illegal drug, and she's straight as an arrow. Kathy is my stabilizer.

When I got to the house, Kathy was happy to see me. What a beautiful home she had, 18,000 square feet and a lovely guest house. After I'd made myself at home I called Nicole.

"Nic, please come up," I begged her. "You don't know how peaceful and safe it feels up here."

But she wouldn't budge. So I settled in. After spending the night there I went back home to get some things. When I walked in, Christian took my car keys away from me and said, "Sit down. There are some things we have to discuss."

Oh, God, just what I needed, a lovers' quarrel. I told him I wasn't going to be staying there that night, that I was going back to Nicole's (which I had decided to do). But he told me I couldn't leave.

"Excuse me," I said. "Are you telling me I'm a prisoner here?"

I walked to the phone, picked it up, and dialed 911. When they answered, I said, "My fiancé has taken my car keys and refuses to let me leave the house. He has no right to do this, and I want police protection immediately.'"

Poor 911. It's probably a call they get countless times on any given night. The dispatcher asked me, "Is the situation such that you literally need a policeman to get you out of the house, ma'am?"

I turned to Christian. "Well, Christian. Do I need the police to release me from my own house?"

Christian sighed, "No, Faye. You don't. But it really would be better if you could stay. Some of our friends are coming over to talk to you."

I hung up the phone and looked at Christian. "I'm going to Nicole's house," I said. "Give me the car keys."

Christian said, "I've just spoken with Nicole. I don't want you going anywhere."

I picked up the phone and called Nicole. "Nic, Christian says he doesn't want me to leave the house and he's talked to you. What's going on?"

"I'll be right over," she said.

Five minutes later, Nicole arrived with Kris and Bruce, Paul, and Kathy Harouche. The minute they walked in the door I knew this was what is called an "intervention." It had never actually happened to me before, but I had heard how it worked from several friends who'd suffered from alcohol or drug problems.

Usually one friend is the "chairman" or "organizer." After mutual discussions with everyone concerned, the chairman decides on the date and the time that the addicted person will be approached in a nonconfrontational way and told: "We love you. Because we love you, we have recognized your problem, and we are here to help you." My chairman was, of course, my dearest friend, Nicole.

It's a searing experience to suddenly find people whose lives you share and whose thoughts are usually open to you suddenly appearing before you for this kind of surprise party. When you're the guest of honor at an intervention, your first impulse is to run screaming from the room. And your first tactic is to deny *everything*!

Even though Nicole was the organizer, Paul and Christian took over as spokesmen. They told me that all my friends had become aware that I needed help. I listened politely, then told them, "Yes, I might have just had a very slight relapse, but I can get back on track very quickly by attending AA meetings regularly."

Just as politely, they told me that I needed to go into full-scale drug rehabilitation. I countered with what I thought was a reasonable offer: I would go to AA meetings at least three times a week. They came back with a compromise position: I would check into the renowned Exodus Recovery Center for just two short weeks.

Nicole held my hand and said gently, "Faye, you know that I've got to help you. You need help. And I need to be strong for you right now, just the way you've always been strong for me. You've always been so good about admitting your mistakes, Faye, and facing things squarely. It's time to do that again and we're going to help you. We love you, Faye. And we want you to get treatment at Exodus."

"Oh, Nic," I said. "I know you're right. I want to help myself, but I get so discouraged sometimes. How can this thing defeat me again? This will be my third time going to rehab. Is it ever going to end?"

Nic smiled and hugged me. "Faye, you know the answer to that, just as well as I do. You have a disease, Faye. It's in your genes. Sometimes the disease comes back, and when it does you need treatment. And if you seek treatment right away every time, the day will come when you'll be able to control the disease all by yourself. You know that. Please, go with us now tonight. We love you. We need to do this now, Faye."

I went through the usual denial with my friends. Then I tried agreeing with them, saying that I should go to Exodus, but I'd do it next week. But they were relentless. They smiled, they nodded, they hugged me, they held my hand.

I was losing ground. And even though I was quietly looking around for an exit, I was truly moved by their concern.

My ex-husband, Paul, was forceful, but wonderful. And even though Christian and I were having insurmountable problems, he was doing his best to act as if our fractured love life had no bearing on my problems. Unfortunately, he didn't do a very good job.

I knew the moment was coming when I'd surrender and agree to rehab. Not yet, though. I said, "Nic, come downstairs for a minute. I really need to talk to you privately."

When we were alone, I said, "Nic, I feel like my hands are tied. I feel like there's nothing I can say. And I can't share what's been happening with anyone but you. Everybody keeps asking me how I got to this point. What bothers me most is that Christian is making me sound as if I'd been on some major drug binge for the last two months. The reality is I've just had two three-day relapses and that's it. Christian is making me sound like I'm Public Enemy Number 1!

Nicole said, "Faye, you're not crazy. And Christian has just freaked out because you want to leave him, and he's blaming it all on drugs. Look, just go into Exodus. I want to have our fun life back again. You've relapsed a little, but don't take the chance. Go now while it's still an easy thing to do."

By now, I was sobbing. "Okay, Nic, I'll go. But this is starting to sound as if going to Exodus will make everything fine. O.J. will stop threatening you, and Christian and I will be happy as clams. Everybody's problems are *not* going to be solved by me going into Exodus."

"No, Faye...but *yours* will be."

* * *

Early the next morning, Christian drove me to Exodus.

Nicole and I shared a dream. We wanted to stop being male-dependent, give up alcohol and drugs, and open up a Starbucks coffee house. After I checked into Exodus, Nicole came to visit me. I was really excited because she had told me she was going to find out how much such a franchise would cost. Nicole had $90,000 in the bank. I had $20,000 in "mad money." We figured we'd have to invest about $40,000 each. I had asked my ex-husband, Paul, to help finance my half of the deal.

When Nicole arrived she said, "Well guess what, Faye? I've checked with Starbucks, and they don't have franchises. So how about opening up our own place?"

That lifted my spirits. Nicole and I spent half an hour talking about the kind of place we'd open. We'd call it Java Café, or something like that. We'd have poetry readings and fabulous teas and coffees. Nicole did cocaine once in a blue moon. She did like her tequila shots, but she vowed that she'd stop all alcohol and drugs completely, right along with me.

"Since you have to go straight, then I will too," she said. "I don't want to make it harder on you."

I laughed and said, "How are we going to go dancing? I can't have any more tequila."

Nicole playfully shook her finger at me. "Remember, we'll have lots of coffee."

"That's fine with me. As long as I don't have to be dependent on any man I'll have what I really want."

"Faye, the day you get out of here will be like our own 'independence day' because O.J. is history. And I don't think you're too happy with Christian either."

Nicole had loved Christian. She thought he was a really wonderful guy until O.J. started manipulating him, getting him on his side. I wasn't very happy with Christian for the same reason. What the hell was it with O.J.? Silly question. He wanted to control the guys so they would control their women and isolate Nicole so she'd be more dependent on him.

After we talked in my room, Nicole walked out to the patio, and I introduced her to some of the other patients. Nicole looked so beautiful that day, people were just staring at her. Everyone kept commenting, "Your friend is so beautiful!" Someone told Nicole that I was always cleaning up and taking care of everybody. Nicole said, "Just wait until she gets totally recovered. It will be really frightening. Faye will organize all your lives and clean all your houses."

Before she left, Nicole brought me a big box of See's assorted nuts and chews. I devoured almost all of them, but I did share a few with some of my new friends. One of them commented on how wonderful Nicole was and how nice it must be to have such a good friend. And I said, "I've had a lot of visitors since I've been here. She's the only one I didn't cry with."

I wasn't embarrassed to have Nicole see me in the hospital. There was such unconditional love between us that all I thought of was the pleasure of seeing her. I felt very uncomfortable with some of my other visitors because they felt compelled to talk about why I was in a recovery center.

That's why my heart sank when it was time to say good-bye to Nicole. I kissed her, we hugged, and she walked away. She turned around and waved once. I never saw her again.

Chapter 20

THE LAST PHONE CALL

SUNDAY NIGHT
JUNE 12, 1994

*A*ll day Sunday, my mind conjured up the image of a pretty little girl dancing—I was missing Sydney's dance recital. Nicole and I had talked about it for weeks. She was so proud. We both kept telling Sydney how lovely she was going to look in her costume and how exciting it would be to appear on stage.

Phone calls had been flying back and forth between Nicole and her parents. The whole family would be there, and Nicole had asked me for ideas on a get-together afterwards. She finally decided on a celebration dinner at Mezzaluna. It was going to be one of those special days that filled you with the warmth of family and friendship. I hated missing it.

Even though it was Sunday, I'd had a busy day at Exodus attending various group sessions. Nicole had left messages for me, and I couldn't wait to call her back. By the time I got out of my last group, it was pointless to call Nicole because she would be at the recital by now. I'd been counting the minutes until I could call her. I knew she wouldn't stay late at Mezzaluna with the kids and family there. She'd probably be home by nine o'clock that evening. That's when I phoned, and she answered immediately.

"Nic, my God, I'm dying of excitement here. Tell me what happened? How did it go? Was Sydney beautiful?"

Nicole was bubbling. "Oh she was so cute. I wish you could have been there. She danced so well, Faye. We were all so proud of her."

"Well, that's no surprise, when she's got a mom who dances like you do. Did everyone have fun?"

"Oh, yeah. The whole family made a big fuss over Sydney. Mom and Dad were the proud grandparents. They just loved it."

"Sounds perfect."

"Well, not quite. I kept missing you today. I was nervous about going to the recital. I knew O.J.

would be there, and I wanted to get your advice on how to handle him."

"What happened?"

"Well, he sat off by himself because he knew I didn't want him next to me. But after the recital, when we were standing around getting everybody together to go to Mezzaluna, O.J. came over. He tried his charm number, but nobody was buying it. Even my mom has finally realized that I've got to get away from him."

"You mean because of the IRS letter?"

"Right."

"So what did you say to him, Nic?"

"Well, when he came over the first time, he said, 'This is our daughter's recital, and I would really like to be a part of it.' And I said, 'O.J., that IRS letter you sent me proved, like nothing else could, that you have no interest in your children.' I told him that there was no way I could force him to leave, but I didn't want him sitting with us."

Wow! Nicole had a tone of voice I'd never heard before. She didn't sound angry—in fact, throughout the phone call, she sounded more happy, confident, and upbeat than I'd ever heard her. But she was speaking of O.J. with a sense of finality, as if he really didn't count anymore. That little soft spot in her heart, that secret place where the strange bond between them had never quite died, was no more. A thrill shot through me. I thought, *My God, she has shaken him forever.*

It was all so brilliantly clear now. Despite everything he'd done to her—the beatings, the humiliations, the other women, the ruthless manipulation of her friends and family in order to isolate her—Nick had absorbed it like a thoroughbred. But now, O.J. had attacked the most precious core of her being: the children she adored. I knew Nicole so well. If you were her friend, a family member, or someone she loved, she was yours to command. She'd do anything for you. She'd listen to your troubles, and if you were the world's biggest pain in the ass, she still loved you unreservedly.

But attack her children? Threaten the security of her precious little Justin and Sydney? Now O.J. was fucking with a tigress, and she'd rip his heart out if he came one step closer to her cubs.

In the wake of the murders, I read press reports of people who'd seen O.J. that weekend—at a dinner party the night before and at other places. They said things like "he was in a fine mood," or "he sure didn't look like a guy who was going to kill his wife." I spoke to Candace and Steve Garvey about that final day. Their children had also been in the dance recital. They knew the real O.J., the man with the public happy, smiling face—and the private face that insiders sometimes see. Candace told me, "He was so despondent, in such a strange state of mind. I've never seen O.J. that way, ever!"

I sensed that something crucial had changed Nicole's heart irrevocably.

O.J. had miscalculated, made a terrible mistake. It was one thing to beat Nicole behind closed doors and have people suspect it. It was quite another to commit himself in writing, for everyone to see, a ruthless threat to report the mother of his children to the IRS.

After the recital, Nicole told me, O.J. again tried to approach her while she was standing with the family as they congratulated Sydney on her special day.

"What did he say, Nic?"

"I don't know. Before he could say much of anything, I told him, 'Fuck off! Get away from us! Get out of my life. You're not welcome with this family anymore.' "

As Nicole spoke, I was shaking my head in disbelief. Had this man so completely lost his center that he didn't realize he'd exposed his total lack of human decency? Typical O.J. again. He had come to the recital under the guise of a doting dad, but his real target was Nicole. Now he'd use anything to regain control of her, to stop her from shaming him publicly by rejecting him again.

I said, "You seem to be handling this really well, Nic. I mean you just told me some pretty heavy stuff, and you really sound okay about it. I'm proud of you. Honestly, I've never heard you sound so good—so peaceful and happy. Now you've got O.J. under control. He'll be leaving town in August. You just have to be really cool about Marcus until then."

The minute I said it, I knew why Nicole was on cloud nine. She'd seen Marcus that day, or she was going to see him. I knew how she got when she was going to be with him, and that's what I think was happening. I asked her, "Nic, are you seeing Marcus?"

She said, "Well, I've seen him."

"Damn, Nic, don't you think O.J. is probably still having you followed?"

"Well, I can't live my life for O.J., Faye. I decided I just can't do that anymore."

I still felt uneasy about Nicole seeing Marcus, but I could tell she didn't want to discuss it anymore. We started talking again about opening our own Java Café. It may sound silly now but it was the hope of a brighter independent life that lifted our spirits. Suddenly, I wasn't in Exodus, and Nic wasn't entrapped in a hellish relationship. We were both able to imagine a happy, warm future. Nic was so glad we were all getting out of unhealthy relationships—Cora was leaving her husband, Ron; Nicole was leaving O.J.; and it was just a matter of time before I would tell Christian it was over. All other problems aside, Nic had not liked his judgmental attitude toward me at the intervention, and I hadn't either.

Nic said, "I'll help you through this, Faye. When I told you that I'd never abandon you, I meant it sincerely. I just want all of us to have a healthy, happy life. Love you. I'll see you tomorrow. Oh, can I bring you something? How about some more See's chocolates?"

I know that I told her I loved her. I've thought a lot about this conversation and have actually attempted to undergo hypnosis to make sure there was no tiny detail that I didn't remember. I really don't think there is; I remember the conversation very well. It was the last time I spoke with the dearest friend I ever had. Somehow I'd love to magically recall the exact words.

But, I'm sure, absolutely sure, that I told her, "I love you." And knowing that helps me a lot.

Chapter 21

EXODUS

*T*here's no good time or bad time to be hit with the shattering news that your best friend has just been murdered. But it's brutal to hear it three days into cocaine treatment. When they called me out of the morning group therapy session and took me into the office of the head counselor, Albert Torres, I knew from his body language that something terrible had happened. I thought, "Why now...when I'm down again?" And then it hit me, in one of those strange, intuitive flashes: *Someone had died.*

Who knows how I knew—but I knew. Perhaps it was because I had felt this way when I lost my sister three years before. Or perhaps it was the so-called paranoia I'd been feeling that danger was stalking my best friend. It had grown so intense in past weeks that Nicole had been convinced that my fears were induced by my cocaine habit.

Who was dead?

Before Torres could speak, I shouted, almost screamed, "Don't tell me! *Don't tell me!*...I can't take this now! I'm trying to get my life back together. I can't hear anything bad. DON'T TELL ME!

For a moment everything stopped. Torres and his staff stood frozen. Then he leaned forward and said quietly, "Faye, please sit down." I couldn't sit. My body went rigid and cold.

"All right, tell me,!" This time I really screamed! The head counselor shook his head slightly, then said, "Faye, it's Nicole..."

"No-o-o....NO! Oh God, not Nic. Oh, Nic..."

A force like I've never felt shuddered through me. The two counselors rushed to grab me as I went into convulsions. I was babbling, shrieking like a wild woman! I said, "It was O.J. He told me he would kill her. Now he has!" I howled incoherently to God, begging him to let Nicole come back. To let her live again. To let me see her. To let me touch her. To let me speak to her and tell her that I love her—before she left us forever.

I ran back to my room. The convulsions lasted for almost two hours. A doctor came. "We want to sedate you, Faye. Please, let us give you something." I could barely put coherent words together. But I told them through clenched teeth, "No, I don't want Valium. I won't take it!"

Finally, I got back control. I asked for details. Then Torres told me the strangest thing: He said Nicole had been shot! And for several hours, that's what I thought had happened. But at that moment it didn't matter how Nicole had died. I knew who had killed her, and now I was afraid I'd be killed for what I knew. "How ironic," I thought. "Nicole put me in this place. She was responsible for my being here. And I should have been there to protect her."

Now, just four days later, I faced the fact that my dearest friend, who had tried so hard to save my life, had lost her own. Slowly, my hysteria turned to control. And then to cold fury. I truly believed that O.J. Simpson had murdered Nicole. It was as pre-ordained as the path of the sun across the sky.

My first response to the tragedy was the thought of committing suicide. It seemed just too much to bear. Perhaps the only reason I didn't kill myself was because I was praying. I was getting down on my knees. I prayed and asked God to relieve me from the bondage of self. I needed to be strong for myself, Francesca, Sydney, and Justin.

I had lost the only unconditional love I'd ever

known—except for my daughter, of course—when Nicole died. While she lived, whatever I did in my life, whatever she did in hers, just didn't matter. Whatever happened, we had each other. It was all about helping each other. And now I just wanted to die.

* * *

STOWE, VERMONT
SEPTEMBER 10, 1994

It all seems like yesterday. And at the same time it seems a hundred years ago.

I miss Nicole perpetually, but she has left me both a legacy and a task.

I have been clean and drug free without exception since I left Exodus, and I will remain so for my daughter, Francesca...and Nicole. I now have two missions. I want to tell the world the truth about my friend and to take a significant part of my revenues from the sales of this book and contribute it to a college fund for Justin and Sydney Simpson.

As always, Nicole is helping me make something of my life.

Thank you, my dearest friend....

Postscript

*T*here's no question that Nicole saved me with the intervention she arranged when she saw that I was losing my battle with drugs. It took time and effort and love, and a lot of nerve, too. She took the time to help me in spite of the oppressive—the unrelenting—fear she had for her own life. Make no mistake. She knew O.J. was dangerous—we all did. And I truly believe that she realized his violence could end in murder. If there is anything salvageable from the bloody scene on Bundy Drive, it is the code-blue alert that has sounded for abused wives everywhere. Maybe it took the sacrifice of Nicole to bring this about.

Every magazine and periodical now carries information on domestic violence. But until recently, it did not seem to be news. In 1985, John Fedders of the Securities and Exchange Commission made headlines when he resigned after it was revealed that he was a wife batterer. And three years later, we read that New York lawyer Joel

Steinberg beat Hedda Nussbaum and struck the blows that killed her daughter, Lisa. Sure, even then it was understood that cases like that were only the tip of the iceberg. But nobody was doing anything about it. Maybe now we will.

After Nicole's death, leading news magazines reported that between two and four million American women are assaulted by a domestic partner—husbands, ex-husbands, and boyfriends—each year. Robert Geffner, president of the Family Violence and Sexual Assault Institute in Tyler, Texas, reports that one in four women will be physically assaulted by a partner or ex-partner during her lifetime, and that abuse cuts across racial, ethnic, religious, and socioeconomic lines.

So it's not just a problem in the inner city, or among the poor, or a particular ethnic group. Domestic violence can—does—happen in every walk of life. The police are called, they come, and, more often than not, leave without making an arrest. They are reluctant to get involved in "family squabbles."

Why did Nicole stay in such a perilous relationship? Why do so many women stay? According to psychologists, there are dozens of reasons: They are afraid to leave, don't know where to go, or—as is often the case—they believe, because they want to believe, the men who say they love them and will never do it again. Elaine Carmen, a psychiatrist at the Solomon Carter Fuller Mental Health Center in Boston, explains, "Eventually, the continued abuse wears down the victims so much that they are unable to leave due to physical and mental exhaustion. The men gradually take control of the women's psyches and destroy their ability to think clearly. The women come to believe they deserve the abuse and that they are incompetent."

Abusive husbands may threaten more violence or even murder to keep their wives from leaving. They threaten to "hunt them down and kill them," says Margaret Byrne, who directs the Illinois Clemency Project for Battered Women. One man, she recalled, told his wife he would find her shelter and burn it down, with her in it. "It's this male sense of entitlement—'If I can't have her, no one can,'" says University of Illinois sociologist Pauline Bart. That's the kind of thing O.J. said to Nicole.

Some women stay "for the sake of the children." But studies tell us that 63 percent of wife batterers go on to be child batterers. And it doesn't stop there. Battered children often grow up to be abusive themselves. So it becomes a sick family tradition. Former Surgeon General C. Everett Koop says, "If you're going to break the chain, you have to break it at the child level." So staying without solid professional help is never an answer.

I can hear it now: What about men who are abused by women? There's no doubt that there are many instances where men are battered by women. According to the Bureau of Justice statistics, about one third of the women in prison for homicide have killed an intimate. But that's another book. This is about Nicole.

Barbara Sachs, executive director of the Council on Battered Women in Atlanta, Georgia, says, "Is there any hope for ending all this violence?" Yes, but not until society recognizes spousal abuse for the crime that it is. Had O.J. Simpson been treated like any other criminal when he previously assaulted his wife, or had his stalking of her been taken seriously, then perhaps two innocent victims would still be alive today.

It's too late for me to help Nicole. I'll never know whether Nicole could have helped herself. But maybe I can help others before it's too late.

There are certain facts every woman should remember:

1. There is never a reason or excuse for anyone to hit you, or hurt you, or subject you to any form of cruelty.

2. No matter how bad it may be to leave, it is much better than staying.

3. If you won't do it for yourself, get out for the sake of your children.

4. You won't be better able to take care of yourself later on. LEAVE NOW!

5. If you don't have a friend or family member to take you in, there are places you can go where you'll be safe and be given an opportunity to make it on your own.

6. You need counseling. If you have no money, there are centers and other resources where you can get it.

7. If you need someone to speak with and aren't ready to tell your friends and family about your situation, you can confide in a clergyman—a minister, priest, rabbi, or other religious leader—a psychologist, or even your physician.

8. Remember, it's his problem, and it's not your fault. But it becomes your problem if you stick around.

9. Even if he promises to get counseling, get out until he's proven that he'll stick to it and until the counselor assures you that he is no longer dangerous to you or your children.

10. Don't wait until next time (and you may be sure there will be a next time.) MOVE NOW!

Please keep the following numbers with you. If you don't get the answers you need on the first call, keep trying. It's not nearly as hard as you may think. It may take awhile, but you can make it. Nicole didn't get out. You can.

Some places for you to call to start getting help and information:

THE NATIONAL ORGANIZATION FOR
VICTIM ASSISTANCE: (800) 879-6682

NATIONAL VICTIM CENTER:
(800) FYI-CALL (394-2255)

THE NATIONAL RESOURCE CENTER ON
DOMESTIC VIOLENCE: (800) 537-2238

NATIONAL COALITION AGAINST DOMESTIC VIOLENCE
NATIONAL OFFICE
P.O. Box 18749
Denver, CO 80218
(303) 839-1852/Fax: (303) 831-9251

MEMBERSHIP/PUBLIC POLICY
P.O. Box 34103
Washington, D.C. 20043
(202) 638-6388/Fax: (202) 628-4899

UNITED STATES
WOMEN'S HELP LINES

ALABAMA
(205) 832-4842

ALASKA
(907) 586-3650

ARIZONA
(602) 224-9477

ARKANSAS
(501) 663-4666

CENTRAL CALIFORNIA
(209) 524-1888

SOUTHERN CALIFORNIA
(213) 655-6098

NORTHERN CALIFORNIA
(415) 457-2464

CONNECTICUT
(203) 524-5890

DELAWARE
(302) 762-6110

DISTRICT OF COLUMBIA
(202) 546-4996

FLORIDA
(407) 628-3885

GEORGIA
(404) 524-3847

HAWAII
(808) 595-3900

IDAHO
(208) 338-1323

ILLINOIS
(217) 789-2830

INDIANA
(317) 724-0075
(800) 332-7385 (state hotline)

IOWA
(515) 281-7284

KANSAS
(316) 232-2757

KENTUCKY
(502) 875-4132

LOUISIANA
(504) 523-3755, ext. 2923

MAINE
(207) 941-1194

MARYLAND
(301) 942-0900

MASSACHUSETTS
(617) 248-0922

MICHIGAN
(517) 484-2924
(517) 372-4960 (state coalition resource library)

MINNESOTA
(612) 646-6177

MISSISSIPPI
(601) 436-3809

MONTANA
(406) 586-7689

NEBRASKA
(402) 476-6256

NEVADA
(702) 746-2700
(800) 992-5757 (state hotline)

NEW HAMPSHIRE
(603) 224-8893

NEW JERSEY
(609) 584-8107
(800) 572-7233 (state hotline)

NEW MEXICO
(515) 526-2819

NEW YORK
(518) 432-4864
(800) 942-6906 English
(800) 942-6908 Spanish

NORTH CAROLINA
(919) 490-1467

NORTH DAKOTA
(701) 255-6240
(800) 472-2911 (state hotline)

OHIO
(614) 221-1255
(614) 221-0023
(800) 934-9840 (state hotline)

OKLAHOMA
(405) 557-1210
(800)522-SAFE (7233)(state hotline)

OREGON
(503) 239-4486/4487

PENNSYLVANIA
(717) 545-6400
(800) 932-4632 (state hotline)

RHODE ISLAND
(401) 723-3051

SOUTH CAROLINA
(803) 232-1339

SOUTH DAKOTA
(605) 624-5311

TENNESSEE
(615) 327-0805

TEXAS
(512) 794-1133

UTAH
(801) 752-4493

VERMONT
(802) 223-1302

VIRGINIA
(804) 221-0990

WASHINGTON
(206) 352-4029
(800) 562-6025 (state hotline)

WEST VIRGINIA
(304) 765-2250

WISCONSIN
(608) 255-0539

WYOMING
(307) 235-2814

CANADIAN
WOMEN'S HELP LINES

BRITISH COLUMBIA: Vancouver Women's Shelter
(604) 872-8212

ALBERTA: Calgary Women's Shelter
(403) 237-8717

SASKATCHEWAN: Isabel Johnson Shelter
(YWCA, Regina)
(306) 525-2151

MANITOBA: Winnipeg Crisis Program
(204) 786-8631

ONTARIO: Education Wife Assault, Toronto
(416) 968-3422

QUEBEC: Montreal Women's Aid
(514) 270-8291

MARITIMES: Bryony House, Halifax
(902) 422-7650